NICHOLAS WRIGHT

Nicholas Wright's plays include *Vincent in Brixton* (Olivier Award for Best New Play, 2003) and the original production of *Mrs Klein*, at the National Theatre, in the West End and in New York; *The Last of the Duchess* adapted from Caroline Blackwood at Hampstead Theatre; *Rattigan's Nijinsky* at Chichester Festival Theatre; *Treetops* and *One Fine Day* at Riverside Studios; *The Gorky Brigade* at the Royal Court; *The Crimes of Vautrin* for Joint Stock; *The Custom of the Country* and *The Desert Air* for the RSC; *Cressida* for the Almeida; and *The Reporter* at the National. Adaptations include *His Dark Materials*, *Three Sisters* and *John Gabriel Borkman* for the National; *Thérèse Raquin* at Chichester Festival Theatre and the National; and *Naked* and *Lulu* at the Almeida, where *Mrs Klein* was also revived in 2009. He wrote the ballet scenario for Christopher Wheeldon's *Alice's Adventures in Wonderland* for the Royal Ballet, the libretti for Rachel Portman's opera *The Little Prince* (Houston Grand Opera) and for Jonathan Dove's opera for television, *Man on the Moon*, based on the Apollo 11 Moon landing. Other writing for television includes adaptations of *More Tales of the City* and *The No. 1 Ladies' Detective Agency* (BBC/HBO). His writing about the theatre includes *99 Plays*, a personal view of playwriting from Aeschylus to the present day, and *Changing Stages: A View of British Theatre in the Twentieth Century*, co-written with Richard Eyre.

Nicholas Wright

TRAVELLING LIGHT

NICK HERN BOOKS
London
www.nickhernbooks.co.uk

A Nick Hern Book

Travelling Light first published in 2012 by Nick Hern Books Limited,
14 Larden Road, London W3 7ST

Travelling Light copyright © Somerset West Ltd, 2012

Nicholas Wright has asserted his right to be identified as the author of
this work

Cover image: Corbis
Cover design: Ned Hoste, 2H

Typeset by Nick Hern Books, London
Printed in the UK by CPI Group (UK) Ltd, Croydon, CR0 4YY

A CIP catalogue record for this book is available from the British Library

ISBN 978 1 84842 247 6

For David

more than ever this time

Travelling Light was first performed in the Lyttelton auditorium of the National Theatre, London, on 18 January 2012 (previews from 11 January), with the following cast:

MAURICE MONTGOMERY	Paul Jesson
TSIPPA	Sue Kelvin
MOTL MENDL / NATE DERSHOWITZ	Damien Molony
JACOB BINDEL	Antony Sher
IDA	Abigail McKern
ARON	Jonathan Woolf
ITZAK	Karl Theobald
ANNA	Lauren O'Neil
JOSEF	Colin Haigh
HEZZIE	Darren Swift
MO	Mark Extance
RIVKA	Alexis Zegerman
JASCHA	Nell McCann, Alexander Semple
ENSEMBLE	Tom Peters, Jill Stanford, Geoffrey Towers, Kate Webster

ACTORS ON FILM

TEACHER	Tom Keller
RABBI	Harry Dickman
ODD-LOOKING WOMAN	Julia Korning
DYING MAN	Michael Grinter
REB GERSHON	Jack Chissick
REB HOROVITZ	Jeffry Kaplow
DOCTOR	Philip Cox
WIFE	Norma Atallah
SERVANT	Jill Stanford
YESHIVA BOYS	Tom Allwinton, Roy Baron, Pablo Carciofa, Daniel Kramer, Henry Markham-Hare, Pip Pearce

Director	Nicholas Hytner
Designer	Bob Crowley
Lighting Designer	Bruno Poet
Sound Designer	Rich Walsh
Video and Projection Designer	Jon Driscoll
Music	Grant Olding

Characters

MAURICE MONTGOMERY, *a film director*
TSIPPA, *Motl's aunt*
MOTL MENDL, *a photographer's son*
JACOB BINDEL, *a timber merchant*
IDA, *Jacob's wife*
ARON, *Jacob's son*
ITZAK, *Jacob's son-in-law*
ANNA, *a servant of the Bindels*
JOSEF, *foreman at the sawmill*
HEZZIE, *a workman*
MO, *a workman*
RIVKA, *Jacob's daughter*
NATE DERSHOWITZ, *an actor*
JASCHA, *a little boy*

Setting

Time: around the dawn of the twentieth century; and 1936.

Place: A shtetl in Eastern Europe; and Hollywood.

Note on the text

Motl and Nate are played by the same actor.

'Maurice' is pronounced 'Maw-reece'.

This text went to press before the end of rehearsals and so may differ slightly from the play as performed.

ACT ONE

Scene One

Film: ocean waves billowing in slow motion.

MAURICE MONTGOMERY *is there.*

He's in his sixties, American/Eastern European. He's dapperly dressed for Los Angeles weather, circa 1936: linen suit, bowtie.

MAURICE. People ask me, 'How did it start?' What was the moment when a moving pattern of light and shade reached through the retinas of my eyes and into my heart? Here's what I tell them. My father had passed away, and I'd gone back to his village to clear up his business affairs. And so I found myself, one evening, in the photographic studio that he had owned for thirty years, playing a piece of film of ocean waves on a Lumière Brothers Cinematograph, vintage 1896. I watched those waves and, believe me, the goosebumps were prickling up and down my arms. What most *entranced* me was how slowly the waves were moving. It seemed quite magical to me. The reason, of course, was the very practical one that the speed of projection wasn't aligned with the speed of the filming, but I didn't know that. I knew nothing about film. I'd never *seen* film! I watched those waves until I felt myself being swallowed up in the moving image. I knew that movies would be my life.

Film ends.

In the darkness: MOTL's aunt, TSIPPA, *is heard.*

TSIPPA. Motl? Motl, are you finished?

Pause.

I'm lighting the lamp.

She does. We're in MOTL*'s father's photographic studio.
Cameras are lying around and photographic portraits are
hung on the walls.* MOTL MENDL *has been projecting the
film onto a space that he's cleared on the wall. He's twenty-
two and wears city clothes.*

Is something the matter? Why are you staring?

MOTL. I'm not.

TSIPPA. Do you want some tea?

MOTL. No, I don't. How long had he had this?

TSIPPA. Not long, not long.

She resumes her knitting.

It arrived two weeks before he passed. He watched the other
moving pictures too. They all came with it. There's one of a
train coming into a station and one of some camels walking
past the Pyramids. Your father was too sick by then to use
the camera.

MOTL. The *what*?

TSIPPA. I said the camera.

MOTL. What camera are you talking about?

TSIPPA. I mean the camera that belongs to it.

MOTL. Is it a *motion* camera?

TSIPPA. Motion?

MOTL. Motion! Movements! *Showing* movements! Is that what
it does?

TSIPPA. What else would it do?

MOTL. Where is it?

TSIPPA. Where?

MOTL. Yes, *where*?

TSIPPA. It's mostly there.

She indicates the cinematograph.

MOTL. What, this is a camera as well?

TSIPPA. That's it as well. But you must put on a different lens. There are some other bits too you have to put inside.

MOTL. So where've they got to?

TSIPPA. Don't ask me. We never got round to it.

MOTL *rummages furiously among the cameras and parts of cameras lying around in a muddle. After a bit:*

MOTL. Auntie, you must have *some* idea. Just *think.*

TSIPPA. Try that box on the table.

It's the handsomely carpentered box in which the cinematograph was delivered. MOTL *finds the alternative lens, and other components, takes them out and begins, by trial and error, converting the cinematograph into camera mode.*

MOTL. I'm going to take this back with me. I don't want anything else.

TSIPPA. When are you going?

MOTL. I'll get the train tomorrow.

TSIPPA. Tomorrow?

She laughs at the absurdity of imagining that a train could arrive so soon.

MOTL. Why are you laughing?

TSIPPA. There isn't a train tomorrow.

MOTL. So when's the next one?

TSIPPA. There's an express comes by on Tuesday, and it could just be that if you talk nicely to the stationmaster, he'll get it to stop for you.

MOTL. Fine, I'll go on Tuesday.

TSIPPA. Why so soon? Stay a bit longer.

MOTL. I do have a job to go to.

TSIPPA. Only a job? You know what I'm asking.

MOTL. No I don't.

TSIPPA. Have you got a fiancée in the city?

MOTL. Oh, I see. No I don't. Not yet.

TSIPPA. You're twenty-two.

MOTL. I know.

He takes a cartridge of film out of the box and inserts it into the cinematograph, ready for shooting.

This ought to work.

Film: a boring, muddy village street. Nothing is happening in it.

MAURICE. Now that I had the *ability* to make a motion picture of my own, the dilemma was, what should it be? Nothing around me matched the timeless majesty of the Pyramids or the ocean. The village was merely a muddle of flooded roads and collapsing roofs.

Film: fields at dawn.

Early one morning I walked out into the fields to capture the delicate haze of dawn. I should have foreseen the problem. Nothing was moving. Until…

Two small dots appear in the air.

… to my excitement, two storks came winging through the sky towards their regular nesting spot on the roof of the community hall. When I developed the film, they looked as small as fleas. However…

Film: TSIPPA harangues the camera, very annoyed.

… ignoring my Aunt Tsippa's protests, I removed the lens from two of my father's cameras to create a telescopic effect, and came back the following day.

Film: two blurry blobs.

It was highly erratic, of course, but when it worked...

The blobs zoom back and forth before settling into a perfectly clear shot of two nesting storks.

... it was miraculous!

End of film.

Scene Two

The shop, a day or two later. JACOB BINDEL, *a strong and ebullient man, is there with his wife* IDA *and their beefy son* ARON, *who is dressed in Orthodox fashion: wide hat, stockings, long coat, etc.* TSIPPA *is listening.*

JACOB. The catcher he saying, 'Where Grabowski? Where Grabowski?' Because the boy have *change* his *name*!

IDA. To Geist.

JACOB. To Geist. So no Grabowski. Only Geist and Geist no good. So now the catcher he go to Reb Mazower, he say, 'I want *your* boy for army.' But Reb Mazower he tell the catcher, 'My boy he gone to America.'

TSIPPA. *Had* he gone to America?

JACOB. He have gone to America! So the catcher he look at list, next boy Rebbetzin Salomon's son. But that boy look sick! He thin like skeleton-boy! For why? Because his mother not feed him only handful of oats like give to rabbit. The catcher he stick him with his finger, he say, 'Is not enough meat, this boy no good for army.' Rebbetzin Salomon, she walk away laughing. Now the catcher he go into the forest, he come to my timber mill.

IDA. Because our boy Aron is at the top of his list.

JACOB. He was at bottom, now is top. The catcher go into barn, he pick up pitchfork, push that pitchfork into hay.

IDA. That's how he found our boy. Aron, you show the lady.

ARON *shows his bandaged leg.*

JACOB. So what I am asking you, Rebbetzin, what we are
wanting is a picture of me and my dear wife Ida and our only
son, with him properly dress like he should be dress before
he put on uniform of the Tsar.

TSIPPA. Believe me, Reb Bindel, I understand you only too
well. When my brother was alive, he took many such
photographs. Come, you can see for yourself.

*She shows them photographs of young men in traditional
dress hanging on the wall.*

But like I say, my brother passed on two months ago, God
rest his soul.

JACOB. You got plenty cameras here. Maybe *you* can take our
photo.

TSIPPA. I only know how to talk to the customers and arrange
the painted cloths. My brother did all the rest.

JACOB. So we come all this way for nothing.

TSIPPA. Wait one moment!

She goes to the door.

(*Calls.*) Motl! *Motl!* (*To the Bindels.*) My brother's only son
has come home at last. He's only just arrived. He has a big
job writing stories for a newspaper in the city.

IDA. You say he's just arrived? Although his father died two
months ago? Why didn't he come home at once? What was
the hold-up?

TSIPPA. It was just a misunderstanding. He's very sorry about
it now.

IDA. Yes, I should hope so!

MOTL *appears, dishevelled. He's been sleeping.*

MOTL. What do you want?

TSIPPA. I want you to take a photo.

IDA *looks at* MOTL *doubtfully.*

IDA. Does he know how?

TSIPPA. Does he know how? Does he know how? Lady, you
don't know what you're asking. He was a brilliant
photographer when he was a boy. But he left home when he
was fifteen. He wanted to make his own way in the world.
That's what he said.

IDA. That's what they always say.

TSIPPA. Motl, why are you waiting?

She digs out a camera.

Here is your father's Eastman Kodak. Give these good
people what they want.

MOTL *takes the camera, dismayed.*

Film: ARON *standing still, looking at the camera like a
mugshot. A naively painted backdrop appears behind him. In
an awkward cut, it's swapped for another.* ARON *looks
bewildered at the camera. He obeys a silent command to
'move', but it looks silly. Cut to* JACOB *and* IDA *having
joined him in shot, and, following instructions from an
unseen* MOTL, *they enact a farewell scene with their son.*
IDA *bursts into genuine tears and gestures angrily at the
camera to go away.*

MAURICE. I had sworn, when I left home, never again to
operate a still camera. But the pressure to do so now was
quite colossal, starting with my aunt's none-too-subtle
reminder that I had sunk so low as to miss my father's
funeral. Because the telegram she sent me telling me that he
was dying went to the wrong address. Because she didn't
have the right one. Because I hadn't written home for
several years. Unwillingly, I took a portrait of the son in his
traditional garb. But when it emerged that I'd been spotted
by the father making a motion picture of the storks, and
when he demanded the same treatment for himself and his

family, I felt bound to refuse. Motion pictures, I explained, were too noble an art to be reduced to the level of family snaps. We argued. I was steadfast. A munificent fee was offered. I accepted it.

End of film.

Scene Three

The shop. A few days later. MOTL *has been showing* JACOB *the film.* MOTL *is dressed for travelling and his luggage is nearby.* TSIPPA *brings in glasses and a bottle.*

JACOB. How many times I see this now?

MOTL (*who is fed up*). You've been watching it every afternoon for the last three days.

He starts to dismantle the cinematograph.

JACOB. Now what you do?

MOTL. I'm packing it up.

TSIPPA. What's the rush? The express won't come till dawn. Will you have some plum brandy, Reb Bindel?

JACOB. Thank you, Rebbetzin, very kind.

TSIPPA gives him brandy.

Motl, you want I take you the station in my cart?

MOTL. That's what you said you'd do.

JACOB. You taking my son away, you know that? It's like I lose him twice.

MOTL. Well, I can't stay here for the rest of my life just to show you a motion picture every day.

No response.

You knew I was going. And you must have known that I'd be taking this with me.

JACOB *gloomily drinks his plum brandy.*

You've got his photo. Isn't that what you wanted? Take it!

He hands JACOB *the framed portrait of* ARON. JACOB *looks at it, dissatisfied.*

JACOB. It not like motion picture. Not so good. You know why? When I am small, small boy, there come fighting in my village. All big fire. All big shouting. My mother, she say, 'Run, Jacob, run.' I run. I come back later, peoples all dead. I walk through river deep to here…

He shows how high the water came.

… I go into black pine forest, sleep in treetop, sleep in badger hole. With badger! Because I only small like so. No talk to peoples, only animals. Come to mountains, live with crazy Jews in caves, we shoot with bows and arrows, we eat wolf and eagle. I learn these people's language, some words only. But come the army, all of these crazy peoples dead in heap.

MOTL. You were telling me why…

JACOB. I walk to Poland, then to Russia, then to nobody know what country. Now I big, I strong, I muscle. Come to here. This village. Not one kopeck to my name, I must be woodcutter-man, I all time hungry. I think my head. I look around me. I see God's green forest that will never go empty. I see a village that will always have need for wood. Oak for beams, pine for floorboards, ash for walls, birch and beech for chairs and tables. I borrow money, I build my sawmill, I pay my debt with interest like honest man. You hear me? Honest man! Now I am boss to twenty labourers, Jews and Gentiles. I am a man of substance. I am respected!

MOTL. It's a remarkable story, but…

JACOB. Story no finish! Story *far* from finish. Story one thousand *versts* from finish! One thing sadness in my heart. You know what is?

MOTL. No.

JACOB. So you no listen to my story?

MOTL. Yes, I listened.

JACOB. Hear nothing funny?

MOTL. Funny about what?

JACOB. The way I talk.

MOTL. Well, yes, I've noticed.

JACOB. What you think?

MOTL. I don't know what to think.

JACOB. Because it different not like you.

MOTL. It's different.

JACOB. You know why? In all my many travel, I never not
learn one language good. Not one! No language proper! God
made his world of words, like it teach in Holy Scripture. But
me, I don't know words. Words for me are like stone wall
around God's world. So I am stranger to God's world. It
close me out! I see with dead man's eyes. I feel with dead
man's fingers. Then I see your motion picture, and the door
to paradise open for me. I see big light, big sun, big sky!
Because no words! No words but all of feelings! Love,
happiness, sadness, tears. I see them clear. I smell them fresh
like apple off tree. It like the words have been scrub clean
from them. I wish I clever man to tell you proper. Only I no
know how.

TSIPPA. That was a wonderful...

There's a knock at the door, which she has been expecting.

Who can this be? I'll answer it.

She opens the door. ITZAK, JACOB's son-in-law, is there.

ITZAK. Rebbetzin Kantor?

TSIPPA. Yes, indeed, I am the aunt of Motl Mendl. Won't you
come in? We're all enjoying a glass of my plum brandy.

ITZAK. Thank you, Rebbetzin.

JACOB. Motl, I want you meeting Itzak. He my son-in-law.

ITZAK *sits, accepts a glass of plum brandy and takes out a folder of papers.*

ITZAK. More to the point, I am Reb Bindel's bookkeeper.

JACOB. He save my business many time.

ITZAK (*to* MOTL). That is a fact I can't dispute. My father-in-law is a truly great human being, but he's too generous for his own good. I hope you realise that nothing he has said to you so far constitutes a contract?

MOTL. What are you talking about?

ITZAK. Don't you know? He wants to make you a proposal.

MOTL. What kind of proposal?

JACOB (*to* ITZAK). Tell him.

ITZAK. But it's *your* proposal.

MOTL. *What* is?

ITZAK. What my father-in-law proposes.

MOTL (*to* JACOB). So propose it.

JACOB. Motl!

MOTL. Yes?

JACOB. You want to make more motion pictures?

MOTL. Yes, I do.

JACOB. What you put in these motion pictures?

MOTL. I'll work that out when I get to it.

JACOB. That fine by me. But you must make your motion pictures in this village.

ITZAK (*to* MOTL). That's his proposal.

MOTL. *No!*

TSIPPA. But it's a very good chance for you!

MOTL. Don't you start! (*To* JACOB.) Reb Bindel, I'm very grateful for your interest. But I'm getting the train tonight. I'm ready to go. There's my cinematograph. My suitcase, hat, umbrella. (*Of a book.*) *The Brothers Karamazov.* That's it. I'm off.

ITZAK. But we haven't discussed the details.

MOTL. There aren't any details! Name a detail!

JACOB (*to* ITZAK). Name a detail.

ITZAK. Will it cost you money to make your motion picture?

JACOB. Good detail.

MOTL. Yes, of course.

ITZAK. How much money?

MOTL. Well, I haven't…

ITZAK. Think!

MOTL. According to the catalogue, the unexposed film is forty-one kopecks a metre.

ITZAK. How many metres would you need?

He listens, clicking on his abacus.

MOTL. Let's say, for twenty minutes of film… at sixteen frames a second…

ITZAK. Can that figure not be reduced?

MOTL. No, it can't!

ITZAK goes on clicking.

ITZAK. … sixty seconds a minute…

MOTL. That can't be reduced either.

TSIPPA. Don't be funny.

ITZAK. How many frames in every metre?

MOTL. Call it fifty.

ITZAK. That comes to… (One hundred and fifty-seven roubles forty-four kopecks.)

MOTL (*interrupts*). Double it.

ITZAK. *Double* it?

MOTL. Technical reasons.

ITZAK *clicks and gets the result. He's appalled.*

ITZAK. Three hundred and fourteen roubles, eighty-eight kopecks!

JACOB. I give it you!

ITZAK (*urgently to* JACOB). May we reflect a moment?

JACOB (*to* MOTL). I give it *all* to you! And then you *stay in the village where you were born.* Where you *belong.* Among the *peoples you belong to.* Your *own peoples*, Motl! Put them all in your motion picture! Every man and woman and child who living here! Then all those peoples will want to see *themselves*!

He indicates the wall.

There on that wall!

TSIPPA. Excuse me, Reb Bindel, but I can't agree. You come here every day to see your motion picture and it's a pleasure to see you and I don't complain. But if all the village is tramping in and out…

JACOB. You right! We change of plan. Peoples stay in their own houses.

ITZAK. But that's not practical! Then Motl must go from door to door with that thing on his back. 'Knock, knock, knock, I've come to show you your motion picture.' 'Oh, kindly wait and have some tea, I'm putting the children to bed.' Wait, wait, wait. 'Oh, now my husband's home, it's time for supper.' House next door. 'Knock, knock, knock…'

JACOB. Enough!

ITZAK. It wouldn't work.

TSIPPA. You'd need a house big enough for everyone.

JACOB. Besides it… (*To* TSIPPA.) What you say?

ITZAK. I said it wouldn't work.

JACOB. Not *you*! The lady. What she say?

TSIPPA. I said it's a pleasure to see you and I don't complain.

JACOB. Not that! No speak! I try remember.

ITZAK. 'You'd need a house big enough for everyone.'

JACOB. That it. That what you need. Big whitewash wall one end, all chairs and benches look same way. Like in community hall! Then all peoples come to see your motion picture *at same time*.

He stares challengingly at ITZAK.

ITZAK. It's an interesting concept. Only how could it be afforded?

JACOB. Peoples *pay* to see it. But not too much. Only what peoples can easily spare. So peoples come in bigger number. And that bigger number pay for bigger and better motion pictures!

ITZAK. So Motl goes around the village with that camera…?

JACOB. He do, he do, he do but he must change his clothes. His clothes no good for clothes. Peoples think he tax collector, they throw stones at him. But my son nice clothes hang up at home with nobody wearing. Motl, what you say?

MOTL. Are you asking me? Do you think I *just might* have an *opinion* on the matter? (*Of* ARON*'s photo.*) I will *never* dress like this. I've got *all* the money I need. And there is *not enough money in the world* to persuade me to stay in this hideous, vile, unbelievably boring village.

JACOB. But you no say 'No'?

MOTL. I *do* say 'No'.

JACOB (*brusque*). So now I take you to the station. Time for you and your auntie say goodbye.

ITZAK *collects some of* MOTL's *luggage and goes out.*

MOTL. But the train doesn't come till dawn.

JACOB. So I must wait for you all night? Who think you are?

He turns away. TSIPPA *approaches* MOTL.

TSIPPA. Motl, will you write to me this time?

MOTL. Yes, I will.

TSIPPA. Don't leave it another seven years before I see you. Who knows if I'll still be here?

MOTL. Don't be ridiculous.

TSIPPA. I'm not going to wait to see you go. It will upset me too much. Kiss me, my darling.

They embrace. She goes, in tears. MOTL *stays, more upset than he would have believed possible.*

JACOB. So now you cry.

MOTL. It's just a *reaction*, right? It's got no *meaning*!

He sits, puts his head in his hands and cries bitterly. After a few moments.

JACOB. You write stories for big newspaper?

MOTL. What are you asking?

JACOB. True or no?

MOTL. I never said they *printed* them. I said I *write* them. Which I *do*. I've written one story that the editor's promised to read *again* if I do some work on it.

JACOB. So what your job?

MOTL. I file the answers to the small advertisements.

JACOB. You got three hundred and fourteen roubles, eighty-eight kopecks?

MOTL *shakes his head.*

You got eighty-eight kopecks?

MOTL *shakes his head.*

If peoples know that you my friend, this village belong to you. Go knock on any door, you say my name, they go fetch hot saucepan, they put food in your mouth.

He looks MOTL *in the eye.*

What you running from?

Film: assorted glimpses of village life, e.g. the main street, with people walking up and down. Yeshiva boys, laughing and waving at the camera. A cow in a field. An ancient rabbi reading to himself from a large tome. Workmen lining up to be photographed outside JACOB's *timber mill. Workmen feeding a log into a circular saw.*

MAURICE. Very typically, the Hollywood producer knows one thing above all others, which is that talent is all that matters. If he gets even the smallest hint of talent in you, he'll swoop down on you and capture you. And then he'll promise you all the world, although it must be said that there's often some more practical figure who restrains his generosity. I discovered this at an early age from a remarkable character in the old country, a timber merchant who was, in a sense, my first producer. He couldn't read or write or even speak with any fluency, but he had a profound understanding of silent film, and this again is typical. Successful producers know their medium. They really do. And luckily for people like me, they work in this wonderful system where they can make their own decisions. They can say, 'I'll back this young man,' or 'I don't give a damn what anyone says, I'll spend this money.' That gives you confidence when you're young. It gives you hope.

End of film.

Scene Four

The shop. It's empty. Dark outside. The cinematograph has been much adapted with cannibalised bits of camera and things found around the house. Strips of film are suspended on a line like washing.

The front door opens and a young woman of twenty-one looks in. This is ANNA. *It's snowing outside and she's bundled up in coat, scarf and boots.*

ANNA. Hello?

She comes into the shop, runs to the fireplace and warms herself at the fire. She's been walking miles and is incredibly cold. MOTL *appears out of the darkroom, carrying bottles of chemicals.*

MOTL. Who are you?

ANNA. I'm Anna.

MOTL. Anna?

ANNA. Anna Mazowiecka. Reb Bindel the timber merchant sent me. He says you need someone to help you.

MOTL. That's you?

ANNA. Aren't you pleased?

MOTL. I wasn't expecting a woman.

ANNA. Well, none of his labourers would be any use to you. I can read and write. I can do numbers. And I'm keen. It'll be much more interesting than what I normally do. Only I've never been so cold in all my life. I think even Rebbetzin Bindel would have offered me some tea by now.

MOTL *glances at the samovar.*

MOTL. The tea's gone out. Would you like some plum brandy? It's not very nice.

ANNA. Yes please.

He finds it and she drinks.

You haven't told me if I've got the job.

MOTL. I haven't decided.

She looks at the cinematograph.

ANNA. Is that the camera?

MOTL. It's the camera *and* the projector.

She comes and looks.

I've had to adapt it quite a lot. My father's old cameras came in useful.

He indicates the tripod.

Tripod.

He swivels the camera right to left.

And I can make it swivel. Couple of things from around the house. Goldfish bowl to absorb the heat.

The goldfish bowl, filled with water and perfectly spherical, stands between the lamp and the projecting mechanism.

Cake-tin lid.

The cake-tin lid stands poised above the projecting mechanism, just where you'd expect a reel of film to be. MOTL spins it and it revolves with a smoothly ticking ball-bearing noise.

ANNA. How does it take the pictures?

MOTL. Are you interested?

ANNA. Mm-hm.

MOTL. Well… the light gradations of the subject strike a sensitised strip of celluloid that passes through the camera as I turn the handle. I take it into the darkroom, soak it in the developing tank, this way up, that way up, so that the darker sections get washed away and the lighter ones remain. You look puzzled.

ANNA. I am. Because if *that's* how it works, then when the lamp shines through it, everything that was black ought to show up white and everything that was white ought to be black.

MOTL. You're right. That's how it looks on the negative.

ANNA. How do you turn it the right way round?

MOTL. I line up the negative with a strip of unexposed film, turn the handle and pass them both through the camera with a light shining through. (*The underside of the cinematograph.*) Back into the darkroom, soak the new film in the developing tank, this way up, that way up, hang it up to dry. All clear?

ANNA. You make a negative *of* the negative?

MOTL. That's one way of looking at it.

ANNA. Is there another way?

MOTL. Not really, no.

ANNA. Do I get the job?

MOTL. I'll give you a try.

She takes off her coat.

ANNA. What do you want me to do?

MOTL. Well, when I'm filming, you'll have to stand at the side and stop people from walking in front.

ANNA. That's all?

MOTL. That's all I can think of.

ANNA. What about these?

She indicates the strips of film hanging everywhere.

MOTL. That's more complicated.

ANNA. Go on.

MOTL. Well, they've all got to be stuck together into one long strip. And some of the strips are rubbish, but I've still got to use them.

ANNA. Why?

MOTL. Because Itzak says Reb Bindel's paid for twenty minutes' worth, so that's what it's got to be.

ANNA. Can't you throw the rubbish away and not tell him?

MOTL. He'll be timing it. I'll show you the kind of thing I mean. I was just about to watch it. Turn down the lamp.

She does, as he lights the limelight behind the projector. In the darkness, he and ANNA are heard but not seen.

I'm going to turn the handle.

He does.

Film: a shop exterior. No one is seen and nothing is happening.

ANNA. What's this?

MOTL. Reb Horowitz the tailor asked me to film the front of his shop.

ANNA. It's boring.

MOTL. It gets worse.

They wait.

Coming up now.

Film: a gentleman in an overcoat comes out of the shop door, sees the camera and waves cheerfully at it.

The door opens, Reb Gershon comes out of the shop and he waves at the camera like an idiot. What do I do with that?

End of film.

A few days later. The shop. TSIPPA is standing on a chair filling in X's on a wallchart of the community hall, which so far looks about half-full. MOTL and ANNA are taking off their coats, having just come in with the cinematograph. Light snow blows in through the door. MOTL is dressed in ARON's clothes: wide hat, stockings, long coat, etc., all too big for him.

TSIPPA. I've been nicely busy while you were out filming. Reb
Schneider wants four places for his children, two for his aunt
and uncle, one for him and one for his wife if her throat gets
better. Though I fear it never will. Motl, you look much nicer
dressed like that.

MOTL. I hate it.

He starts taking off his clothes.

TSIPPA. You'll get used to it.

MOTL. I will never get used to it! Not in a million years! I feel
grotesque!

He goes into the kitchen to change. ANNA *goes to the work
table. Glue, a notebook and a lens for magnification stand
ready, and very long strips of film are suspended above the
table.*

TSIPPA (*calls to* MOTL). Reb Bindel called by this afternoon.
He wants the motion picture ready by Wednesday night.

MOTL *appears, half-undressed, in the doorway.*

MOTL. What for?

TSIPPA. He wants his family to see it one night early.

MOTL. Why?

TSIPPA. Don't ask me. But if you take my advice, you'll do
what he wants. It's him who's paying.

MOTL *disappears to finish changing.* TSIPPA *gets off the
chair.*

(*Calls.*) Motl, I'm going to stay at my sister's tonight, I'm
leaving now.

MOTL (*calls*). So?

TSIPPA. So?

MOTL. *So?*

TSIPPA. So must I leave you and the young lady alone
together?

MOTL. Auntie, please! She's my *assistant*!

TSIPPA. And what a big difference *that* must make. Goodnight.

ANNA. Goodnight, Rebbetzin.

MOTL. Goodnight!

TSIPPA. Goodnight.

> TSIPPA *goes.* MOTL *reappears in his usual clothes.*

MOTL. I'm sorry about my aunt.

ANNA. I don't mind.

MOTL. She can't believe that a man and a woman can be alone together and not think about anything except work.

ANNA. Yes, I've noticed.

> MOTL *goes to his workbench and fiddles with a lens.*

Why do you think we've got to show it one night early?

MOTL. I've no idea. It must be some kind of rustic ritual.

ANNA. We'll have to work all night.

MOTL. Can you do that?

ANNA. Oh yes. I won't be missed as long as I'm back by dawn.

> *She goes over to his table to get something, then looks at the little mechanism he's working on.*

What are you doing?

MOTL. I'm looking for a way to get close up to the subject without changing the lens.

ANNA. Is that what the outer ring is for?

MOTL. Mm-hm.

> *She jiggles it back and forth.*

ANNA. Far away… close up.

MOTL. What do you think?

ANNA. Won't it make people feel a bit sick, zooming in like that?

MOTL. I don't see why.

ANNA. It's just that…

MOTL. What?

ANNA. Nothing.

She moves away, looking at the photos on the wall.

Will you go back to the newspaper when we've finished?

MOTL. No, they sacked me when I didn't show up.

ANNA. You'll have to make another motion picture.

MOTL. That's the plan.

She stops to look at a photo.

ANNA. There's a photo of Reb Bindel here with his wife and children. It must have been taken years ago. The sawmill's only just been built and the children are babies.

She looks more closely.

They had a dog.

MOTL. Look at the family in the photo next to it.

She does.

ANNA. They had a dog just like it.

She looks at another photo.

There's another one here. Oh, they're all the same dog.

MOTL. It's my dog Samson. He used to love having his photo taken. He'd wait until my father was just about to press the button, and then he'd scamper around and stand in the middle wagging his tail.

ANNA. You looked quite happy telling me that.

MOTL. I was. I mean, I was when I had the dog.

ANNA. Why did you run away from home?

MOTL. I didn't *run*. I *left*.

    ANNA *is about to start work.*

    Leave that for a minute. I want to see if this does what I think it will. Sit on that chair.

    She does. He brings the cinematograph over.

ANNA. Like this?

MOTL. That's right.

    He moves the lamp so as to light her better.

    In a moment I'm going to turn the outer ring and come in close.

    He looks through the device.

    Look this way. Not *at* me. Over my shoulder. That's it. Now turn your head very slowly to the right and smile. Not too much. No, that's a grin.

ANNA. You're making me nervous.

MOTL. All right, go back as you were.

    She resumes her pose.

    Slowly this time. Turn. Just turn.

    She slowly turns her head while he changes focus on the lens.

    And back to me.

    Pause.

ANNA. Well?

MOTL. You're right about the zooming-in. It's awful. But when I came in closer…

    Pause.

ANNA. How much closer did you get?

MOTL. It was just your face.

He looks at her, puzzled.

Hold on a minute.

He goes over and moves a lamp so as to light her differently. Glances at her again, still puzzled, then goes back, checks through the device.

What are you thinking about?

ANNA. I'm not thinking about anything.

MOTL. Well, go on doing it. Turn again. A bit to the left. And back.

Her eyes fill with tears. He stands.

Are you all right?

ANNA. I'm fine. I just hate not thinking about anything.

He's still looking at her.

How did it look?

MOTL. It was very surprising.

ANNA. Can I get on with what I was doing?

MOTL. Yes, do.

ANNA. Do you remember that ridiculous bit you showed me, where Reb Gershon comes out of the door? I think I've thought of a way to fix it.

MOTL. Good.

He watches her with vastly increased interest as she searches among the strips of film. After a few moments:

How long have you and I been making motion pictures?

ANNA. Almost a week.

MOTL. So tell me… what do you do at Jacob's timber mill?

ANNA. I cook, I clean. I read to Rebbetzin Bindel, I write her letters for her. I do the things that they can't do on the Sabbath.

MOTL. Like what?

ANNA. Lighting candles. Posting letters. Cutting bread.

She looks at him, amused.

Didn't you know that I'm not Jewish?

MOTL. I hadn't thought about it.

ANNA. Really not?

MOTL. No, not at all. I think who's Jewish and who isn't is one of those things you ought to get over in adolescence.

ANNA. I don't think anyone gets over it.

MOTL. I did.

ANNA. How?

MOTL. By asking questions.

ANNA. Like?

MOTL. Like... 'Poppa, what does it mean to be Jewish?'

ANNA. And he says what?

MOTL. He says, 'Well, my son, there are Jews who don't even believe in God, so being Jewish is not a religion. And there are Chinese Jews and Abyssinian Jews, which proves that it isn't a race. So if you want a speedy answer to this complex question that has baffled many great minds before you, I would say that if somebody *thinks* they're Jewish, then that's what they are.'

ANNA. So what do you say?

MOTL. 'Then, Poppa, I've got bad news for you. I don't think I'm Jewish.'

ANNA. Big shock?

MOTL. No, not at all. He says, 'That's very interesting, my son, why not?'

ANNA. And you reply?

MOTL. 'Because I'm a unique human being with thoughts and impulses and intellectual ambitions that can't be *categorised* in such a limiting way.'

ANNA. What does he say to that?

MOTL. He says, 'But that's how Jewish you are! It *proves* you're Jewish!'

He laughs, then tears come to his eyes.

ANNA. Did you love him?

MOTL. It seems I did.

He gets out his handkerchief, blows his nose. She looks among the strips of film and finds what she's looking for: the section of Reb Gershon coming out of the tailor's shop. He watches her.

Where did you learn to read and write?

ANNA. In the convent.

MOTL. Were you born in the convent?

ANNA. Nobody's *born* in a convent. My mother left me on the doorstep in a cardboard box and ran away. I've no idea who my father was. Some passing soldier, I expect. The nuns taught me Russian and Polish, I learned Yiddish at the timber mill and I'm studying English.

MOTL. What for?

ANNA. For when I go to America.

MOTL. When will you do that?

ANNA. As soon as I can. Wouldn't you go to America if you could?

MOTL. I was planning to.

ANNA. What happened?

MOTL. I discovered motion pictures.

ANNA. Don't they have motion pictures in America?

MOTL. I'm sure they do, but I don't suppose they're very advanced.

ANNA has found what she was looking for.

ANNA. This is the other bit about Reb Gershon. Come and look.

MOTL sits next to her and she holds up the film for both to see.

He's walking down the main street looking very pleased with himself. You wanted to try out the swivel so, as he gets closer, you swing around and you follow him into Reb Horowitz's tailor's shop.

MOTL. Same place that he came out of.

ANNA. He goes there every day, because their children are getting married. Let's get started. Has your auntie got any scissors?

MOTL. What for?

ANNA. So I can cut the film.

MOTL. *Cut* it?

ANNA. Yes. I want to cut it and rearrange it.

MOTL. You can't! You'll ruin it!

ANNA. No, I won't. It'll all be fine. Just get me the scissors! Go on!

She examines the strips of film, selecting the sections she wants to cut. Meanwhile, MOTL looks for the scissors.

MOTL (*muttering*). She's out of her mind. She's mad.

He gives her the scissors. She holds them, poised.

ANNA. Shall I?

MOTL. Do it.

She cuts into both strips, taking out the two Reb Gershon bits.

ANNA. Now I can put the two Reb Gershon bits together, and then it will look as though we *meant* it to be like that.

MOTL. Right.

ANNA. You think so?

MOTL. Yes, I do. I see what you mean.

ANNA. But where should the new bit go? First or second?

MOTL. Well, I filmed it the following day, so it ought to be second.

ANNA (*doubtful*). I can try it. Pass me the glue.

She sticks the strips together. He watches her, getting closer until he is paused in the long, suspenseful moment before he might kiss her.

Don't do that.

MOTL. I'm not doing anything.

ANNA. Yes, you are and I don't like it. Go further off. I want to look at this properly.

She does.

It isn't right. Take a look.

She passes the strip to him, he looks at it and they pass it back and forth.

He comes *out* of the shop…

MOTL. And then?

She snaps the dressmaking scissors in the air.

ANNA. Then he goes back *in*. It's stupid.

She passes it to him and he looks at it.

MOTL. He could have forgotten something and gone back to get it.

ANNA. I hadn't thought of it like that.

MOTL. But I still don't like it.

ANNA. Nor me.

She thinks.

I've got it.

MOTL. No, *I've* got it. We'll change them round.

ANNA. That's it.

She takes the two strips of film, eases them apart and sticks them together the other way round. Looks at them.

MOTL. Well?

ANNA. He goes *into* the shop…

MOTL *snaps the scissors in the air.*

MOTL. Cut!

ANNA. … and he comes out.

MOTL. Just like anyone would.

She examines it.

ANNA. But it still doesn't work.

MOTL. Why not?

ANNA. Well, it just doesn't, and the reason's very peculiar. Let's look at it properly.

MOTL *feeds the film into the projector.*

Put out the lamps.

He puts out the lamps. She turns the handle.

Film: Reb Gershon walks jauntily down the main street of the village and is seen, in a bumpy pan, going into the tailor's shop.

ANNA. Reb Gershon goes into the shop. It was sunny that day, so he's wearing a jacket.

It's clear from MOTL's voice that he's physically close to her.

MOTL. And?

Film: Reb Gershon comes out of the shop, as seen before.

ANNA. You filmed this bit the day before, when it was colder, so he's wearing an overcoat. Watch it again.

Film: she runs the same piece of film backwards.

You see? If he wasn't wearing an overcoat when he went *in*… then he can't be wearing one when he comes *out*.

They're beginning to sound distracted.

MOTL. You're… right.

ANNA. So what do we do?

MOTL. We could go back and…

ANNA. … film it again?

MOTL. They'll never pay for it…

End of film.

But the lights stay out. In fact, it's darker now. Dead blackout. There's a pause, accompanied by some rustling and bumping. Then all that can be heard is breathing and a gasp.

Later that night. MOTL *and* ANNA *have been making love.* ANNA *is awake.* MOTL, *who is asleep, wakes and looks at her. Half-dressed,* ANNA *wraps a blanket loosely around her and looks out of the window.*

ANNA. It's nearly dawn.

Unabashed, she collects some clothes and starts getting dressed.

MOTL. I'll walk back with you.

ANNA. No, don't. I love being in the forest at night. Just me and the foxes.

He stares at her half-nakedness.

MOTL. I can't believe you're walking around the room like that.

ANNA. Would you rather I didn't?

MOTL. I love it. I just didn't know that women do that. But then I don't know much about women. Do you know much about men?

ANNA. I don't know anything at all.

She continues getting dressed.

MOTL. I'm going to write to Jacob. You can read it to him in the morning. I want him to pay for my next picture. He won't refuse. He loves me. Doesn't he love me?

ANNA. I think he does.

MOTL. I know he does. Only there's something I'm not going to tell him until he agrees. You've got to be in the picture. It's got to be all about you. I'm going to insist on that. Because…

He falters.

… because there's something about your…

Pause.

… when I saw you through the lens… I knew it had to be you.

He embraces her and kisses her. She disengages gently.

ANNA. Go back to bed.

MOTL. I will in a minute. I want to fix up the overcoat bit.

ANNA. Don't be annoyed but… while you were asleep, I found a tiny piece of film that we hadn't used. I pasted it in between, and it works quite well.

She indicates the cinematograph.

It's in there.

MOTL *goes to the cinematograph, illuminates the projector and cranks the handle.*

Film. Jaunty klezmer-style music, as for a silent movie. Reb Gershon comes down the street and the camera follows him into the tailor's shop.

MAURICE. Here's what I saw. Reb Gershon approaches down the main street. I follow him round, he goes into the shop and… Cut!

Film: inside the tailor's shop. Reb Horowitz holds up an overcoat and smiles to somebody off-camera.

Inside the shop, Reb Horowitz the tailor holds up an overcoat and smiles at Anna, of whom all we can see is her shoulder at the side of the frame. It could just possibly be Reb Gershon's shoulder.

Film: Reb Gershon comes out of the shop and waves at the camera.

Cut! The door opens and Reb Gershon comes out, wearing the overcoat that he appears to have *bought in the tailor's shop*!

Film: credits and 'The End', all in Yiddish in Hebrew lettering. Meanwhile:

What I was looking at, on the wall of my father's photographic studio, was no less than the first example of dramatic montage in the entire history of cinema! How had we done it? How had a twenty-two-year-old… pretentious layabout, quite frankly, in an unknown shtetl, along with a Gentile housemaid, made a discovery that would elude every other cinematic pioneer for years to come? It was inspired by love. Hers and mine. What else could it be?

End of film.

Scene Five

The shop. Wednesday night. MOTL has been projecting the film onto the wall. The room is crowded. JACOB, IDA, ITZAK and ITZAK's wife RIVKA are in the audience. RIVKA is smartly dressed and much bejewelled. TSIPPA is there with a live chicken. ANNA starts passing around drink and cakes. JACOB's foreman, JOSEF, has been watching along with two other workmen, HEZZIE and MO. HEZZIE has no legs but can move around with agility on a little wheeled platform.

JACOB. Why so quiet? Show your feelings!

He applauds and others join in, though clearly not entirely convinced.

Motl, come where peoples can see you. This is the wonder-boy! Let me kiss you, wonder-boy!

He kisses MOTL, to louder applause.

Do you know what I see in my mind? Friday morning, peoples take me by my collar, they have tears in eyes. They say to me, 'How is it, Jacob, we have a wonder-boy in our village and it take you to find him?'

IDA. Except they won't all like the picture.

JACOB. No, of course they not all like! Why you think I show it one night early?

He gestures to one at a time.

It is so you, and you, and you can say to Motl what is wrong with his motion picture, and he work late tonight and fix it better.

MOTL (*shocked*). What?

JACOB. You heard.

MOTL. But, Jacob, I've been working *day and night* on this, and there isn't a *single thing* that isn't *exactly* the way I want it!

JACOB. Look these peoples! These are same as peoples who come tomorrow night! They *think* the same. They *feel* the same. They say to their neighbours *exactly* same. So take that cross look off your face and do to your motion picture what they tell you. Peoples, come!

They take up positions for a discussion. Meanwhile:

ITZAK. It's the same principle as the tailor fitting a suit on the customer before it leaves the shop.

MOTL (*rebellious*). Brilliant, brilliant.

JACOB. Who first to speak? Josef?

IDA (*annoyed*). Why Josef first?

JACOB. Who give me better advice than my own foreman? He is smart, smart man. Mo here, he not so smart. Hezzie here, he most smart of all, except one time he get little bit drunk and fall asleep on the sawmill. Josef, say to Motl what you no like.

JOSEF confers with HEZZIE and MO.

MOTL (*whispering to* ANNA). This is torture.

JOSEF is ready to speak.

JOSEF. What me and the men didn't like at first, sir, was when it went so fast from one place to another.

MO. It made our brains feel all mixed up.

HEZZIE. But then we remembered, sir, that when we dream at night, we go from place to place like that.

MOTL. Well, that's an extremely perceptive comment. Motion pictures and dreams are very alike.

IDA. Maybe that's why Rebbetzin Abramsky fell asleep.

Laughter. All look around at the sleeping guest.

JACOB. She was tired! She was exhausted! She chop wood all day and then her husband beat her like a carpet. What you expect but that she fall asleep?

MOTL (*anxious*). When did she fall asleep?

IDA. It was when the blacksmith put a horseshoe on Reb Leibowitz's horse and then he put on three more horseshoes. I was nearly falling asleep myself. If you had come to me and asked, before you made your motion picture, I would have said four horseshoes is three too many.

RIVKA. Add some variety.

JACOB. You hear what my beautiful daughter Rivka say?

MOTL. Yes, well, a blacksmith's life doesn't have that much variety.

RIVKA. We've got a right to our opinions!

IDA. We're the people who have to *see* your motion picture.

MOTL (*incensed*). Like you've got no choice? Like people are forcing you?

ANNA *kicks his ankle and takes away his glass.*

Look, I hear what you're saying and that's enough with the horseshoes. Hasn't anyone got something more constructive to say?

JACOB (*to everyone*). You hear what he say? What else was bad about the motion picture?

RIVKA. I didn't like it when it showed Reb Sacks.

MOTL. Why not?

RIVKA. Because I didn't.

MOTL. Could you be more specific?

RIVKA. How?

MOTL. Well, was the scene in the baker's shop too long?

RIVKA. No, not too long.

MOTL. Wasn't it clear that he was making bagels?

RIVKA. Of course it was! You think I've never seen a bagel?

MOTL. So what was the problem?

RIVKA. I don't like *him*.

IDA. He sold her a pie and she found a mouse in it.

MOTL. Just to get some clarity here, are we talking about real life, or are we talking about a motion picture?

IDA. Nobody likes Reb Sacks and that is that!

MOTL. Thank you, that's really helpful. No more nasty people in motion pictures.

IDA. You mean there'll be *another* motion picture?

JACOB. Please, we talk about that later. (*To everyone.*) What else, what else? We're doing nice.

TSIPPA. Well, there was one bit, Motl, that I'm very surprised that you included. I'm sure that everyone knows what I'm talking about.

MOTL (*shocked*). Auntie!

IDA. Yes, that was shocking.

MOTL. You mean the washerwoman, right? That's what she wears all day when she's down by the river. If she didn't, she'd get the rest of her clothes all wet.

IDA. It was her *blouse* that got all wet. That was a big problem.

JOSEF (*facetiously*). It was *two* big problems.

The workmen laugh and the women glance at them with irritation.

MOTL. Don't you think it's rather hypocritical to get somebody to do your washing for you, and then complain because...?

JACOB. Motl, please. I want a motion picture that is suitable for my family. They don't want see no big gazungas. Take them out.

MO. I wish it was *her* who took them out!

The workmen laugh raucously.

IDA. For shame, for shame!

MOTL. Great, I'll remember that in future. All young ladies to be totally covered up.

IDA. What is this 'future'? Tell me, Jacob!

JACOB. One thing one time. What else did nobody like?

ITZAK. Well, speaking personally, I was disturbed when Rabbi Meltzer appeared in such an incomplete condition.

MOTL *puts his head in his hands.*

MOTL. I don't believe this.

JACOB. Why you complain? Hezzie is no complete and he my best workman.

IDA. But Rabbi Meltzer was not just missing his *legs*. He had no legs, no arms, not even a body.

RIVKA. Just a face and that was all.

IDA. Like he'd had some horrible operation.

MOTL. That was *a close-up*! I wanted to show the tranquillity in his eyes! The lines of experience etched on his wise old face! Look, this is a *new* and *radical* kind of art. If it disturbs you, maybe you ought to ask *yourselves* why you've got *stuck* in your *dreary, conventional expectations*...!

His words are drowned in a chorus of disagreement and ANNA discreetly takes his glass away.

Listen, listen! Wasn't there one bit, towards the end, that had your full attention? Well?

IDA (*speaking with reluctance*). I will admit, it was good when Reb Gershon bought an overcoat.

There's a murmur of agreement.

RIVKA. Except he didn't really buy it.

ITZAK. It wasn't even the same overcoat.

MOTL. But you liked it!

IDA. Nobody said that the picture didn't have some nice moments in it. But that's not to say I would want to see it again.

JACOB sighs in disappointment.

JACOB. Still, we done our best. Motl, you made a very nice picture here…

ITZAK. … a very *artistic* picture…

JACOB. … only I sorry to say that nobody else agree.

ITZAK. Even an artist cannot argue with his public.

MOTL. Well, if we're talking about the public…! (*To* TSIPPA.) Auntie, give me that.

She has been holding the seating plan, rolled up. He takes and unrolls it, revealing that it is now entirely covered in X's.

This is what the community hall will look like tomorrow night. It will be *packed*. In fact we've probably made a profit. Itzak? Isn't that so?

ITZAK. I was wondering when you'd ask.

He rises and opens his ledger.

The hall will be full, and that is undeniable. What complicates the matter is that so many of the customers chose not to pay in cash. We have, let's see…

He indicates a pile of assorted goods and continues in a satirical tone:

… one sack of turnips, several pairs of boots, one boy's pullover, two buckets of milk, seven bottles of vodka, six dozen eggs, one broken scythe…

TSIPPA holds up the chicken.

TSIPPA. Mr Bookkeeper!

ITZAK. ... Oh, and I nearly forgot, one chicken.

JACOB. Tell us the money.

ITZAK. The money again is problematic because of the wide
variety of currencies used, not all of which are viable.

JACOB. Yes, yes, how much?

ITZAK *consults his ledger.*

ITZAK. One hundred and eighty-four roubles, forty-five
Austrian marks, fifty-two Lithuanian crowns, three American
dollars and thirty-four Polish zlotys.

JACOB. Plenty roubles!

ITZAK. Only before expenses are deducted.

MOTL. What expenses?

ITZAK. Chemicals, postage, use of the cart...

JACOB. I throw that in.

ITZAK (*with resignation*). You'll throw that in. I'll turn to the
hires.

MOTL. Hires of what?

ITZAK *flips through his ledger to the appropriate page.*

ITZAK. One cow, fifty kopecks.

MOTL. That was Jacob's cow! It didn't even *do* anything. It just
stood in a field!

ITZAK. But it was in the motion picture!

MOTL. I *know* it was in the picture! I *made* the picture and now
the *cow's* getting paid and I'm *not*!

ANNA *again removes* MOTL's *plum brandy.*

JACOB. Forget the cow. I throw in the cow. Look, I not stupid.
Maybe to break even in this motion picture business not so
easy like I thought. But Jacob Bindel never a man to give up
hope. There must be a way...

RIVKA. A way to what? To make *more* motion pictures?

IDA. That's what I keep asking to the air.

JACOB. One more. Just one. Because this wonder-boy he write me so nice a letter.

IDA. He wrote a letter? That you cannot even read! Jacob, you are too trusting. Please, I'm begging you, no more motion pictures!

RIVKA. Listen to Itzak. He's a practical man.

ITZAK. Although a practical mind is not devoid of imagination.

RIVKA. Meaning what?

ITZAK. I have a plan in mind, by which a motion picture could pay for itself.

IDA. He's gone crazy too.

JACOB. So what's your plan?

ITZAK. Let us look at our village as a crane might do when it's flying above us, bent for warmer climes…

JACOB. But what is plan?

ITZAK. I'm coming to that. What does it see, this crane, as it gazes down upon the forests and plains and mountain peaks? What else but twisting pillars of smoke arising from the multitudinous chimney stacks of villages just like ours? Belzberg to the north, Ozer across the river, Glintz a short day's ride beyond it…

ALL. The plan! The plan!

ITZAK. I'm talking multiple showings. Motl can show his motion picture in each one of these villages, and sell the tickets many times!

MOTL *explodes with enthusiasm.*

MOTL. That's it! He's got it!

He kisses ITZAK *on both cheeks.*

Thank you, Itzak, thank you! We'll put the camera on the cart and go to Glintz and…

RIVKA. Oh, screw your heads back on!

IDA. If there's one thing the butcher in Glintz does *not* want to see, it's the butcher here who he doesn't even talk to.

RIVKA. And their innkeeper hates our innkeeper, and their rabbi hates our rabbi…

MOTL. So you know what I'll do?

Uproar: nobody wants to know. They just want him to go away.

Listen to me! I'll make a picture about people who don't exist. Who *never* existed.

There's a bewildered silence, and a few voices mutter: 'What?'

An *imaginary* butcher, an *imaginary* baker, whatever I need. Then nobody can object to them. I'll show it in every village for miles around. In every *town*. As far as *Kovna*.

JACOB (*prompting him*). And the picture have a story.

MOTL *stares at him.*

MOTL. Have a story?

JACOB. Like Reb Gershon's overcoat. Why you surprise? I thought you already say it have a story?

MOTL. I *meant* to, yes. It's got a story about… ah…

Thinking fast, he catches sight of ANNA.

… a girl. A beautiful, innocent girl. Who gets into trouble with a soldier. And when her father finds out that she's expecting a baby, he throws her out of the house. We see her trudging through the storm, with the wind and the snow beating against her face, all the way to the orphanage. How's that for a story?

TSIPPA. What happens to the baby?

MOTL *thinks fast.*

MOTL. It grows up in the orphanage and becomes…

ANNA *catches* MOTL'*s eye and does mopping-the-floor actions.*

… a servant to *the very same family* who threw her mother out into the snow. So, Jacob, obviously there's some filling-out to do, but the *framework*'s there, the *basic theme*, and I honestly think…

RIVKA. Does the mother die?

TSIPPA. I hope she doesn't.

MOTL. No, no! No! She becomes…

He looks at ANNA, *who signals that she has no idea.*

… a famous opera singer. But in spite of her huge success and the, the…

RIVKA. … parties every night…

MOTL. … the parties and the, the…

RIVKA. … . bouquets of flowers thrown onto the stage…

MOTL. … there's still a terrible *pain* in her heart because of the dear little daughter who she gave away.

IDA. So then what happens?

MOTL. Well, one night… a lady from the orphanage comes to the opera house.

JACOB. Who this lady?

MOTL. She's…

IDA. … I think, a kindly, generous lady who gives her money to the poor. She says, 'Go home at once…

She looks anxiously at JACOB.

… Your father has had a fatal heart attack.'

MOTL. And so the woman, that's the singer…

RIVKA. ... wraps herself in her luxurious furs and calls for her coach...

MOTL. ... her coach, that's right, drives back to her village for the funeral and we...

He snaps his fingers in the air.

... 'cut' to the father...

JACOB. And he still alive! He lie in bed, his family round him and the rabbi chant a prayer. The old man rest his head on pillow, close his eyes...

RIVKA *sings a few bars of a sentimental parlour song.*

IDA. What's this singing?

RIVKA. It's his daughter, outside the window in the snow.

ALL. Ah!

RIVKA. The old man asks, 'What's that I hear?' They say, 'It's only a gypsy passing by. Go back to sleep.'

JACOB. But he call out, 'No, no! I know what is! It is an angel come to lead me to a better world.'

ALL. *Aah!*

RIVKA. He opens his eyes. He sees his daughter by the side of his bed, and she's holding the little girl by her hand. She says, 'Here is your long-lost granddaughter, who's been living with you for all these years. Beloved father, do you forgive me now?'

TSIPPA (*tearful*). Oh no!

JACOB. The old man eyes all tears. He say, 'It is not you, but I who must be forgive.' He rest his head...

MOTL *takes centre stage to apply the final button.*

MOTL. ... and then a radiant light shines down on his face from Heaven. And he dies.

Silence. Finally IDA *speaks.*

IDA. That was one beautiful story.

TSIPPA. It truly was, it truly was.

JOSEF. When she was walking through the snow, I thought of all the girls I've treated badly.

He chokes with sobs as the other workmen comfort him.

ITZAK. Everybody I know would want to see that motion picture.

JACOB. You know what it called?

He draws a big poster in the air.

'The Singing of the Angel.'

General agreement.

MOTL (*to* JACOB). So what do you think?

JACOB. I like it.

MOTL. You *do*? You *like* it?

He embraces JACOB. General appreciation and applause.

JACOB. Time for home! All peoples into cart!

People start to leave.

TSIPPA (*addressing* IDA). That woman must be your beautiful daughter Rivka.

ITZAK. She'll be perfect! (*To* RIVKA.) Won't you, my sweet?

RIVKA (*who has long ago decided the same thing*). Oh, do you really think I'm good enough? I'll do my best.

MOTL watches in dismay as they go. TSIPPA has taken dishes into the kitchen.

MOTL (*to* JACOB). Jacob, we need to talk.

JACOB. So talk.

MOTL. This picture has got to be made the way I want.

JACOB. So what you think I am wanting too? I want a *Motl Mendl* motion picture. Nobody else's!

MOTL. So the part of the woman…

JACOB. … but with the woman, maybe you no get what you want.

MOTL. But the woman is *crucial*. She's the *emotional centre of the story*! She needs a special quality of *vulnerability* and *innocence*, and there's only one person I know…

JACOB. Yes, but I no want opera woman to be my daughter.

MOTL stares at him.

MOTL. *Not* your daughter?

JACOB. No.

MOTL. Then *who*…?

JACOB. It must be Anna.

MOTL. *Anna?*

JACOB. I make surprise for you?

MOTL. You do.

JACOB. Sit by me.

He pats a chair beside him and MOTL sits.

No think badly of me for what I tell you now. I no bad man. I do my best to making a decent life.

Tears are in his eyes. He looks round at the kitchen and lowers his voice.

But when I look at that girl she poke the cobwebs or she carry that tray of cookies, I like eighteen again. I like tree in springtime with hot sap like kettle rise into every branch. You hear my meaning?

MOTL. I think I'm getting the rough idea.

JACOB. If we give Anna this big nice thing to do, I think she find it in heart to be good friend even to ugly old man like me.

MOTL. Mm-hm.

JACOB. You know what I mean, 'good friend'?

MOTL. I can imagine it.

JACOB. I think she will be 'good friend'. I think she will make me one big happy man. So here is my one… my one…

MOTL. … condition…

JACOB. … yes, condition. Anna must act that opera woman, or there will be no motion picture. Now what you say?

MOTL *wrestles with this moral crisis for about half a second.*

MOTL. She'll be perfect.

ANNA *comes in, having been sent to hurry* JACOB *up.*

ANNA. They're all waiting.

JACOB. Yes, I coming.

He embraces MOTL.

Goodnight.

MOTL. Goodnight.

JACOB *goes.*

ANNA. Well?

MOTL. He'll pay for the picture.

ANNA. That's what I thought he'd do. I'd better go.

She kisses him and goes. MOTL *is left alone. He goes to the cinematograph. Examines it, touches it. The sound of* TSIPPA *clattering in the kitchen dies away and a different atmosphere is felt.*

MAURICE *comes in through the outside door. He looks at* MOTL, *still at the cinematograph.*

MAURICE (*quietly to himself*). It's how it was.

End of Act One.

ACT TWO

Scene One

1936. The photographic studio, now a half-assembled set in a Hollywood film studio. MAURICE examines the cinematograph, just as MOTL was doing when last seen.

NATE DERSHOWITZ appears at the door. He's twenty-two, Jewish, working class, from Brooklyn. He carries a script.

NATE. Mr Montgomery? It's me. Nate Dershowitz.

MAURICE. I know who it is. Come in.

NATE does.

NATE. I'm sorry I'm late. I got called in to see the Studio Head.

MAURICE. What did he say to you?

NATE. He didn't say anything. He did a sort of a soft-shoe shuffle behind his desk…

He demonstrates.

…then he came walking towards me with his hand held out, only just as he got into shaking distance, I could see him thinking, 'If I get any closer, this guy's gonna ask me a favour,' so he rang for his secretary and she showed me out.

MAURICE. The man's a cliché. Don't quote me. This is what I wanted to show you.

(*Calls into the studio.*) Okay, boys. Can you put everything in place?

Stagehands assemble the set. He and NATE are looking at it.

(*To* NATE.) What do you think?

NATE. It's amazing.

MAURICE. It is, it is. There are marvellous craftsmen working in all the studios now. I walk on to the set and there's some fine antique. But newly made. I say, 'Bring me the man responsible, I want to shake his hand.' So in the lunch break, some quiet little fellow comes sidling up to me, a Mr Finkelstein, let's say, he's newly arrived in America, he 'no speak so good', he comes from three generations of cabinet-makers in Berlin. But now the business has been stolen by the Nazis, and so on, so on. So there we are. One gets one's advantages from the misfortunes of others. Sad but true. Now I'll show you something else.

He takes over the cinematograph and loads film. Meanwhile:

Allow me to say, I'm never wrong about such things, and I know for a fact that you'll be tremendous in this part. I knew it the moment I saw you in New York in that terrible play. What a title! Boy oh boy. *A Man Must Eat.* But in the middle of all this tedious political schtick, on you came and everything clicked for me. So where are you from?

NATE. I'm from Brooklyn.

MAURICE. That's a tough neighbourhood to grow up in.

NATE. It sure is, Mr Montgomery. I was big in a street gang myself for a while. I only got into acting because of a girl. Then, like you saw in my CV, I won a scholarship to an acting course with Mr Lee Strasberg.

MAURICE. Mr Strasberg? I've heard good things about him, and I've heard bad things too, but it seems that nothing he taught you did you too much harm.

NATE. There's nothing can harm my acting, Mr Montgomery, because there ain't nothing else that I can do.

MAURICE (*appreciatively*). I believe you. Has the studio settled on a name for you yet?

NATE. 'Nick Driver.'

MAURICE. 'Nick Driver.'

He thinks about this for a moment.

I've heard worse. You know, one of the first big jobs I had
in this industry, the Head of the Studio called me in. I'd
done the fight scenes for the film of a theatre play, and
they worked so well that, don't think I'm boasting, but
they more or less took over the whole picture. He says,
'Young man, I like your work, but I don't like the credit
they've given you.' I say, 'It's news to me I've got a credit,
what is it?' He reads out from this piece of paper, '*Romeo
and Juliet* by William Shakespeare, additional scenes by
Motl Mendl.' That is the day that Maurice Montgomery
was born.

He turns on the limelight.

Limelight.

(*Calls.*) Lights!

Darkness.

Now watch.

*Film: an odd-looking young woman with flowers in her hair
comes running out of a house.*

This I don't know why she's here. It's some village girl who
married a demon. Nobody *saw* the demon. It must have
flown away. It left a note on her pillow.

*With a look of horror, she holds up a tattered and singed
piece of paper.*

That's it.

Film: ANNA *walks through heavy real-life snow, holding a
baby.*

This is my first day's shooting on my very first feature, you
could call it. This is Anna.

NATE. She had something.

MAURICE. Oh, she did.

Some inquisitive children run into shot. JOSEF *appears and
chases them away with a stick.*

NATE. Were you in love with her?

MAURICE. You know what I was? I was obsessed with the way
she looked on screen. I used to say to her, it was as though
there was a light underneath her skin. One could see right
into her soul. Like she'd invented a new language that
everyone in the world could understand.

*Film: cut to the photographic shop, now kitted out as a
studio. ITZAK holds up a card displaying the title of the
film: it's in Yiddish in Hebrew lettering.*

MAURICE. Deathbed scene. Don't try to follow it in your
script. Just watch.

*A heavily made-up man – the aged father – lies in bed
surrounded by 'wife', 'doctor', 'rabbi', 'servant girl' with
broom and whoever else.*

Budget problems.

*MOTL and ITZAK are having a stand-up row, filmed by
some mischievous person who's got hold of the camera.*

*Next: the workmen put new scenery into place. It represents
a theatrical dressing room. We see JACOB directing
activities, pointing and shouting.*

And now the trouble begins.

Film ends.

Scene Two

The shop, kitted out for filming, as just seen on film. JOSEF *and*
MO *bring in a dressing table and then go round fixing whatever
else needs it.* HEZZIE *buzzes about on his trolley.* TSIPPA *is
sewing a floor-length cape,* ITZAK *is writing in his ledger and*
IDA, *respectably dressed as the visitor from the orphanage,
reads a newspaper.* RIVKA, *elaborately dressed, checks her
appearance in a mirror.*

MOTL (*calls*). Has anyone seen Anna?

JOSEF (*shouts*). Quiet! Quiet!

MOTL. Josef, you don't have to shout like that. Where's Anna?

HEZZIE. She's with Reb Bindel in her dressing room, sir.

MOTL. Well, find them at once and tell them we're trying to
    start.

HEZZIE. I do it, sir.

   He whizzes across the floor on his trolley and out.

MOTL. Josef, I need to arrange the reflectors. Rivka, can you
    take a seat at the dressing table?

RIVKA. Sure, no worries.

   She does, as the men arrange a pair of reflective devices.

MOTL. Auntie, how's the cloak coming on?

TSIPPA. It's fine, don't rush me.

   RIVKA *is in position.*

MOTL. Rivka, can you look a little bit forward? Now to the left.

   She turns to the right.

   Other left. Josef, up a bit. Down a bit. Rivka, is that what
   you're going to be wearing?

RIVKA. Why not?

MOTL. Well, isn't it rather elaborate for a dresser in an opera house?

RIVKA. You mean a dresser doesn't know how to dress?

MOTL. Yes, of course she does, but I think of this one as a modest, reliable woman who probably can't afford a pair of diamond earrings.

IDA. Don't nag at her.

TSIPPA. Yes, leave her alone.

MOTL. Well, just as long as they're off for the filming. Josef, mark it there. Thank you, Rivka, that's all I need.

RIVKA. So glad to be useful.

She steps down. JACOB *comes in, holding up his watch and tapping on it, followed by* ANNA.

JACOB. Time to start! Time to start! Why no one ready?

He sees the dressing table.

Motl, what this?

MOTL. It's the dressing table, Jacob.

JACOB. Yes, I *see* is dressing table but is poor person's one! This woman is famous opera singer, she must have big rich dressing table. Josef, go to cart, bring my daughter's dressing table.

JOSEF *and* MO *take away the dressing table.*

MOTL. Jacob, I think the dressing table we've *got* will…

JACOB. Motl, we no talk dressing tables, yes? I cannot eat no lunch for worry.

MOTL. What's the matter?

JACOB. What the matter? What the matter? People will come to see my movie, *Singing of the Angel*, what do they hear, *no singing!*

MOTL. That's the nature of the medium, Jacob.

JACOB. No excuses! We say 'singing', we must give them singing. When Anna singing in the snow, my beautiful daughter Rivka…

He beckons her into his orbit.

…she stand at side with big light on her, she sing beautiful song for all to hear.

MOTL. Fine, let's talk about that.

JACOB. No talk, we do it. Itzak, show me the who-does-what.

He joins ITZAK, *who produces a stack of caption cards.* MOTL *is stunned.*

MOTL (*to* ANNA). Did you see that? He sent the *dressing table away.*

ANNA. Didn't he like it?

MOTL. Who *cares*? The dressing table's nothing to *do* with him. It's *not his film.* I'm struggling here. I suppose at the back of it all there's some, I don't know, some kind of folksy patriarchal thing going on, but I can't handle it. It's driving me mad. What were you doing with him in your dressing room? Did he…?

ANNA. No, he did not! He's never laid a finger on me. He's much too shy.

MOTL. Too shy for *what*?

The penny drops.

My God, is *that* what you thought I meant?

He laughs.

No, what I *meant* was, was he telling you how to play the scene?

ANNA. He had a couple of suggestions.

MOTL. Ignore them. Don't pay any attention to anything he says. Just listen to me and nobody else.

He sees JOSEF *and* MO *bringing in a more ornate dressing table.*

Right, let's start.

TSIPPA *approaches* ANNA *with the cloak.*

TSIPPA. Will you try this on, my dear?

She hangs it around ANNA *and fixes her hair and make-up.* MOTL *gets to work detaching the camera from its tripod. In time he will give it to* HEZZIE *and check that* HEZZIE *can operate it. Meanwhile,* ITZAK *has been showing* JACOB *the caption cards.*

JACOB. Show me again.

ITZAK *wearily holds up a card.*

ITZAK. 'The Singing of the Angel.'

JACOB. I take your word for it.

Another card.

ITZAK. The list of who impersonates which character.

JACOB. Go back to the start.

ITZAK *sighs and produces another card.*

ITZAK. 'Jacob Bindel…'

JACOB. I can read my name.

ITZAK. '… presents to you…'

JACOB. Next card.

The next card:

ITZAK. 'A Motl Mendl motion picture.'

JACOB *studies it thoughtfully.*

Jacob, won't you tell me what the problem is? I can see there's something on your mind.

JACOB *indicates first* MOTL's *credit, then his own.*

JACOB. That one more small. That one more big.

He sees ANNA *in her cape.*

Look, look! The singing angel! Peoples will think a star has fall to earth! Anna, you sit and rest yourself. Big scene to come.

He looks at the new dressing table.

(*To the men, unheard by* MOTL.) No good, no good.

The men take it away. Meanwhile:

MOTL. Can I have quiet for a minute, please? Where is Polonsky?

ITZAK. Who did you say?

MOTL. Polonsky the fiddler. Why isn't he here?

ITZAK. I'm very sorry to tell you, Motl, but the man's a shark. He wanted more for one day's filming than for two weddings and a bar mitzvah. I felt obliged to save the money.

MOTL. Itzak, we've talked over and over about the fiddler. He's *essential* for the *mood*.

ITZAK. Yes, yes, but…

MOTL. How the *hell* do you expect Anna to play this *sensitive* scene if nothing's happening to evoke her emotions?

ITZAK. Motl, please! You make me nervous when you get excited. Polonsky recommended another fiddler. He should be here. It isn't my fault he's late.

MOTL. Well, I'm not waiting.

He takes the centre of the room.

Quiet, everyone.

He notices that the dressing table has gone.

Oh no. Oh no. Where's the dressing table?

JACOB. I send it away. My wife's is better.

MOTL. But, *Jacob*, the one we had *before*, the one we *started* with, was…

JACOB. No talk dressing table! Is motion picture we are making! Why has Hezzie got the camera?

He indicates HEZZIE, who does indeed have the camera and is looking through the lens.

MOTL. It's for the special shot.

JACOB. What special about it?

MOTL. You'll see in a minute. Once we've got the furniture back.

The men bring in a yet more ornate dressing table.

Wonderful. Wonderful. Put it there! Nobody move it! *No one!* Great, that's fine! Can I have everyone's attention, please?

JOSEF. Quiet! Quiet! Quiet for the movie!

MOTL (*to* JOSEF). All *right*, all *right*!

IDA (*to* TSIPPA). I don't like the workmen calling it a 'movie'.

TSIPPA. I agree. It isn't dignified.

She takes RIVKA's jewels off her.

MOTL (*addressing everyone*). This afternoon I want you all to concentrate as hard as you can because, and I'm not pointing a finger at anyone, but it seems that, owing to some misguided sense of economy…

TSIPPA *slyly indicates* ITZAK.

… we only ordered enough film to do every scene once. Josef…

JOSEF. Sir?

MOTL. … you're going to the station tonight to collect the new delivery, is that correct?

JOSEF. Yes, sir.

MOTL. And the express *is* going to stop? Is that quite certain? Itzak, have you talked to the stationmaster?

ITZAK *is adding up figures.*

Itzak!

ITZAK. I have talked to him at length.

TSIPPA. I hope you have, because we don't want another mess-up like with the fiddler.

ITZAK (*irate*). Are you talking to me, Rebbetzin Kantor?

TSIPPA. Yes I certainly am!

ITZAK. Do you see this box?

He holds up a metal box.

This is all the money we have to spend. There is no more. I repeat, *no more*! If you were paying for the fiddler yourself…

TSIPPA. Pay him myself I'd rather do than…!

MOTL. Can we do this later?

JOSEF (*very loudly*). Quiet! Quiet!

MOTL. Josef, *please*. (*To everyone.*) The scene is a dressing room in the Imperial Theatre, St Petersburg. Jacob, if you sit there you're going to be in it.

JACOB *moves his chair a little further out.* TSIPPA *puts the finishing touches to* ANNA's *clothes and make-up.*

Rivka, you stand at the dressing table arranging things.

RIVKA. When I did it before, I was sitting down.

MOTL. You were standing in for Anna.

RIVKA. I was 'standing in for Anna'? Fine, I'll do some arranging.

She arranges things on the dressing table noisily and with no good grace.

MOTL. Anna, you'll come in through this door.

He marks a spot on the floor.

Hezzie, you'll start from here. Have you been practising?

HEZZIE. I got it perfect, sir.

MOTL. Anna, you wait outside.

She goes out of the door.

Lights.

JOSEF *plugs in the lamp.*

JOSEF. Light on.

MOTL. Is everyone ready? Concentrate. And…

There's a moment of quiet.

…Hezzie, camera!

HEZZIE *cranks the camera.*

HEZZIE. I'm turning the handle round, sir.

MOTL. Anna! Go!

She comes in.

You've just come offstage. You pause for a moment to relive the triumph of your performance.

ITZAK *holds up a caption card.*

ITZAK (*reading out*). 'Tonight I sang as never before.'

MOTL (*to* ANNA). Now, very slowly, walk around the dressing table. Hezzie and Mo, get moving.

ANNA *walks to the dressing table while* MO *propels* HEZZIE *on his trolley so that together they perform a tracking shot.*

Don't bump it, Mo. Gently, gently! Anna, you go over to the coat stand… Rivka, you join her… Help her take off her cape, very slowly, very elegant… And you turn away from her to hang it up… And then go back around the dressing table.

RIVKA *does so, favouring the camera with a wide smile.*

JACOB. No look back! Rivka, no look at camera!

MOTL. It's all right, Jacob, she can't be seen there. (*To the actors.*) That's where I'll '*cut*' the film.

The actors relax. MOTL *takes the camera from* HEZZIE *and replaces it on the tripod. Meanwhile:*

Oh, and Jacob, it might be less confusing for everyone if I'm the one who tells them what to do.

JACOB. Motl, Motl, why you fight like so?

He ruffles MOTL'*s hair.*

Nobody doubt you clever boy. But where your wisdom of life? Where you keep it?

He taps MOTL'*s trouser pockets.*

Not in that pocket. Not that pocket. I no clever man, but I know *people's* wisdom like must go into movie. I been starve no food. I been chains around my ankles. I been flog on my back. You want see?

He's about to take off his jacket and shirt, but MOTL *stops him.*

MOTL. I'm only saying, whatever you think, just tell me first.

JACOB. I do it.

MOTL. Promise?

JACOB. Sure I promise.

MOTL. Fine. (*To everyone.*) Listen, everyone! I want, very quickly, to see Rebbetzin Bindel coming in through the door…

IDA. That door got stuck last night, if anyone's interested.

MOTL. I know it did, that's why we're trying it now. Positions, please!

Actors take up their positions.

Rivka, you open the door... Rebbetzin Bindel comes in...
Yes, just like that... Anna, you see her, and you remember
the terrible tragedy that happened... And now she's going to
bring you some bad news.

JACOB (*to* ANNA). Not like so! Not like so!

MOTL (*to* JACOB). Tell *me*, tell *me*!

JACOB. So listen good. When Anna see my dear wife Ida, Anna
must smile.

MOTL. Smile?

JACOB. Yes.

MOTL. Are you quite sure about that?

JACOB. Yes.

MOTL. But she's... ah... meeting the woman she gave her
beautiful little baby away to at the orphanage. Wouldn't that
make her sad?

JACOB. I say it simple for you. From this lady, Anna will get
bad news. So she must smile before she get it.

MOTL. Why's that better?

JACOB. Motl, no be stupid boy! Sad face one, then sad face two
is nothing change. Is no *surprise* for peoples looking.
Peoples must have surprise, you no see that?

MOTL. I'm only...

To everyone's amazement, JACOB *picks up a chair, waves it
wildly above his head and screams.*

JACOB. Ah! Ah!

MOTL. Jacob, put down that chair.

JACOB. Ah! Ah! Ah!

MOTL. If you don't put it down, I'm going to...

JACOB. What you do? What you do?

MOTL. Just put it down. You're upsetting people.

JACOB *puts down the chair.*

You were saying *what*?

JACOB. I show you.

He colourfully demonstrates the emotions that he's talking about.

'Now I happy, now I sad.' Is better, yes? Is good surprise. Other way round, is also better. 'Now I sad, oh, now I win the lottery!' *Big* surprise. No argue. Do like I say. Why you stand like donkey? Time is pushing.

MOTL (*shaken*). Fine, let's, um, let's…

JACOB. Practise it from start.

MOTL. Yes, fine, let's do that. Rebbetzin Bindel, can you be ready to try the whole scene, please?

IDA. I've been ready all day.

She gets into position, taking her newspaper with her.

MOTL. Anna and Rivka, can you go back to your first positions? Ready? Rivka, you go around the dressing table and you pick up the card and you give it to Anna with a…

ANNA. … sympathetic look.

RIVKA. But who's it from?

ANNA rolls her eyes.

MOTL. It's from the woman who runs the orphanage, like it's always been. She left the card for Anna at the stage door. So you tell Anna…

ITZAK holds up a caption card.

ITZAK. 'There is a lady outside who runs an orphanage…'

JACOB. And then lady walk through door! So then we know what lady! Card is useless. Throw it away.

ITZAK resignedly tears it up.

MOTL. Oh, for God's sake! Let's just shoot it. Is everyone ready? (*To the actors.*) Back to your places. Josef, get what light you can.

He turns the crank.

I'm turning the handle. Go!

RIVKA *gives* ANNA *the card with a tragic look.*

Keep it subtle, Rivka. Anna, you read the card.

IDA. I can't read it from here. How's anybody going to know what's written on it?

ITZAK. Hold it up, my darling! Hold it up!

MOTL. No, no, I'm going to insert a close-up of it. Don't stop, don't stop! Anna, you make a sign to Rivka to show your visitor in.

ANNA *does.*

And, Rivka, off you go. No, go! Go. *Go!* Anna, look quickly in the mirror. Your hair, your face… Rebbetzin Bindel, in you come.

IDA *moves into shot.*

Anna, you see her. Rebbetzin Bindel, you're amazed by how she's changed…

JACOB. Anna, smile!

MOTL. … You see her magnificent clothes…

JACOB. Anna famous opera singer now!

MOTL. Rebbetzin Bindel, clasp her hands…

JACOB. Anna, happy!

MOTL. … And now you tell her that her father is dangerously ill.

JACOB. Anna, *sad!* Anna, *sad!*

MOTL. You say how sorry you are to bring bad news… and out you go. Cut. Take a rest everyone. I've got to reload.

He does so, with his hands plunged into a box with a light-proof cover.

JACOB. We do it again.

MOTL. No, we don't.

JACOB. But I no feel it. Not one piece! I want to suffer it in my heart.

ANNA. Motl, I'd love another chance.

MOTL. No, look, I'm sorry, but we've got less than an hour of daylight left. Maybe tomorrow I'll do a close-up. And, Jacob, for the millionth time, *don't interfere!*

JACOB *subsides into a black sulk.*

JACOB. Good, fine, I sit.

He sits. MOTL *catches sight of a very small boy,* JASCHA, *who has just rushed in, as if late for school, carrying a violin case.*

MOTL. Who's that?

JACOB. You asking me? How do I know? I just the fool who pay the money.

ITZAK. This is the fiddler, just in time!

MOTL. But he's a *little boy!*

ITZAK. So?

MOTL. Itzak, don't you know what the fiddler's *for*? It's for when Anna thinks about her father. He has to evoke her loving memories! And her fear that her father is going to die! We need a first-class violinist!

ITZAK. Well, this boy's mother says he's better than Polonsky.

TSIPPA. *That* I believe.

ITZAK. Little boy, get ready.

JASCHA unpacks his violin.

JACOB. Can I speak? Am I permitted? How peoples know that Anna she thinking father?

ITZAK *nervously holds up a card.*

ITZAK. 'Your father is gravely ill'?

JACOB. I hate those cards! They horrible cards! Where your respect for peoples who no can read?

IDA. I can read and I wouldn't know what Anna's thinking.

JOSEF. She could be thinking about the egg she have for breakfast!

He and the other workmen have a good laugh at this.

ANNA. I've been worried about this too.

MOTL *gives her a look of fury at this treachery.*

JACOB. No worry, I got idea. Show Anna thinking, then her father his face, in air above her! Two faces both! And father his face is fuzzy and soft around, like father in dream. Then peoples know she thinking father!

MOTL. *How* do I do that? *How?*

ANNA. What if...

MOTL. *What?*

ANNA. Well... do you remember the time you used the same film twice?

MOTL. Yes and I *ruined* it!

ANNA. *How* did you ruin it?

She demonstrates:

It showed somebody *there.* And somebody *there.* And the second somebody was all fuzzy and soft around. Do you see what I'm saying? Film it *once* and then film it all over again with...

MOTL. Look, I know what you're saying.

ANNA. And?

MOTL (*begrudging*). I suppose it just might work.

JACOB. Who know best! Who know best?

He stands and raises his fists like a champion, to general applause.

MOTL. All right, let's go. You ready, Anna?

ANNA. Can I hear the music first?

MOTL. I think that's probably wise. Play, little boy.

JASCHA *stands with his arms folded.*

I said *play*!

JASCHA. I'm not used to playing under these circumstances.

JACOB *leaps to his feet.*

JACOB (*yells*). Play, or I break your fingers!

JASCHA *concentrates furiously and plays a snatch of folksy music. He's nervous but he's pretty good all the same.*

RIVKA (*disparagingly*). He's no Polonsky.

MOTL. Fine, that will do. Settle down, everyone. Lights.

JOSEF *and* MO *plug in the lights.*

JOSEF. Lamp one.

MO. Lamp two.

MOTL. Anna, I want you to get up slowly, look upwards in that direction…

ANNA. Motl, do me a favour. Leave it to me.

MOTL. I'm getting used to this. All right, I'm turning.

He cranks the handle.

Go.

JASCHA *concentrates furiously, then improvises a rhapsody of astonishing virtuosity and beauty.* ANNA *responds with a silent show of grief.* MOTL *watches, entranced.* JACOB, *noticing this, stares at* MOTL *with growing suspicion.*

Film: ANNA *continues the silent, solo scene described above. Different viewpoints of her dissolve into each other. Meanwhile* JASCHA*'s beautiful accompaniment continues.* MAURICE*'s voice is heard:*

MAURICE. Nobody knew that little boy's name. But many years later, as I was sitting on my own in the Hollywood Bowl, watching Jascha Heifetz play Tchaikovsky's Violin Concerto in D Major, I felt an uncanny sense of familiarity. Behind the maestro's austere and hawk-like features, I seemed to discern the chubby face of the child who had coaxed such marvellous silent acting from the woman who, once upon a time, I had thought I loved. He *could* have been Heifetz. Heifetz was born and raised not far away. But how many Jewish children in that time and place could conjure enchantment out of a cherry-red violin? Perhaps many thousands. Of whom some found other things to do in their future lives. Of whom others were forgotten. Of whom some would die of typhus, cholera, tuberculosis. Of whom one survived.

Scene Three

The shop. That night. ANNA and MOTL are making love in the bed used for the filming. Suddenly ANNA starts up.

ANNA. Ssh! Listen.

MOTL. I can't hear anything.

There's a banging on the door and JACOB's voice is heard.

JACOB. Motl!

ANNA. Don't answer.

MOTL. He knows I'm here.

More banging and JACOB is heard again.

JACOB. Motl!

MOTL. He'll wake up the whole street.

He gets up and dives into some clothes.

TSIPPA (*calls from her bedroom*). Who's that? Who's that?

MOTL (*calls*). It's all right, auntie, I'll get it.

ANNA slips out of the bed and goes out of sight.

(*Calls.*) I'm coming, Jacob.

He unlocks and opens the door. JACOB is there with a bottle.

JACOB. You still awake? I sorry you so bother.

MOTL. No, no, it's fine. Come in.

JACOB. You have some drink?

MOTL. Why not?

JACOB makes for the kitchen.

JACOB. I get us glass.

He gets a glass, while MOTL *snatches up any evidence of* ANNA *that's been lying around.* JACOB *looks searchingly round the room and pours brandy for them both. They drink.*

MOTL. Did you just… happen to be passing by, or is there something you want to say?

JACOB. I walk through forest. Thinking, thinking, always thinking. What do we film tomorrow?

MOTL. It's all in the schedule, Jacob.

JACOB. It good schedule. But there is 'Nothing so good… that it cannot be make better.' Who say that?

MOTL. Well, basically I think that almost anybody could have said it.

JACOB. You angry with me?

MOTL. No.

JACOB. Maybe I whip you too hard today.

MOTL. I wouldn't say that. We're just a volatile creative partnership.

JACOB. Nice way to say it! That is *educated* way. But, Motl, in motion pictures, education only one leg of the mule. No make your movie for professors. No, no, no. Make it for ordinary peoples. They must laugh and cry and they must feel it in their hearts. You know how a movie reach to heart?

He points to his mouth.

Not through this.

He points to his ears.

Not through these.

He points to his eyes.

Through these. The eyes. Always eyes. You know why I understand so good the movies?

MOTL. Tell me.

JACOB. Because my eyes can read the words in…

MOTL. ... What?

JACOB *searches for the word.*

JACOB. ... in... 'Ssh!'

MOTL. In...?

JACOB. 'Ssh!'

MOTL. In silence?

JACOB. Yes, in silence. I look at a man his face, I know if he speaking true, I know he lie.

MOTL. That must be a useful talent.

JACOB. Very useful.

Pause.

MOTL. So...?

JACOB. So, Motl, tell me. What is Anna to you? No say in words. I look. I see. I know.

Pause.

MOTL. Could you remind me of the question?

JACOB. Is Anna a woman of flesh and blood for you?

He puts a finger on MOTL*'s lips.*

No speak!

He looks intently at MOTL.

Or...

MOTL. ... Is she...?

JACOB. ... Is she only a moving picture on the wall? No talk! I look. I look at you now.

He examines MOTL*'s face intently. Then he bursts into a sigh of relief and embraces* MOTL *passionately.*

You tell true! I was a bad man to suspect you! Motl, I love you! You like my son to me! We make more movies years and years to come!

MOTL. Sounds good.

JACOB *pours more plum brandy for them both.*

JACOB. One story that I am thinking, in this village, old-time rabbi have one daughter, she deaf and dumb, he pray to God, God fix her better. You like?

MOTL. There's a lot of potential there.

JACOB. Another story often told. The Cossacks come to village, kill all kinds of peoples. Nobody strong to fight them. Then come a man who is bravest of all Jews. One day he kill seven Cossacks in the main street and the rest all ride away. What we call that movie?

MOTL. *One Man Alone*?

JACOB. You see? You clever like this. Another story. Boy and girl are working in kosher butcher shop and there is always quarrel between them. Each one put in newspaper, 'Please somebody write to me, I wanting love.' Each one get answer say, 'You sound very nice, I want we meet for glass of tea.' Each one go to teahouse same time, same place, and what you think come next?

MOTL. They fall in love and they get married.

JACOB. Is stupid story?

MOTL. It's a delightful story. Jacob, I don't want to rush you, but we've got an early start tomorrow.

JACOB. It good that we make more movies. You know why?

MOTL. Why?

JACOB. I will die and you will die, but our movies live for always. If in one hundred years, this village be only mud once more, and peoples who live in it dead and gone and nobody know our names, a Jew can look at our movies and he say to his children, 'Children, listen. These are the stories what we told each other. They made our hearts beat side by side like single heart. It how we lived. It how we were. It how it was.'

He clasps MOTL*'s hands.*

We make good film in the morning.

MOTL. Yes, we will. I promise we will. Goodnight.

JACOB. Goodnight.

> JACOB *goes.* ANNA *comes cautiously out.* MOTL *glances guiltily at her.*

MOTL. What?

ANNA. Is it true? Is that what you were thinking? That I'm just a moving picture on a wall?

MOTL. I wasn't thinking anything. It's all in his mind. I think he's clinically insane. Does he seriously, honestly think I can go on *working* with him after the way he *behaved* today? And the horrible joke of it all is that I *created* him! I *did*. I took this jolly old salt-of-the-earth Tolstoyan type and turned him into a fucking monster. He's like the Golem. His huge clay feet are stomping all over me.

ANNA. Calm down.

MOTL. I won't. Why should I? Why should I spend the rest of my fucking life making *Jewish fucking movies*! I never *intended* movies to be like this. They were meant to be noble, miraculous things, like stormy oceans and birds in flight. But then *people* and *money* got involved and it all turned into 'Boo-hoo-hoo' and 'Ooh, what happens next?' And I can't get away from it. Unless I...

ANNA. What?

MOTL. Unless I go to America. That's it. That's what I'll do. I'll make the movies that I *believe* in. Because there won't be Jacob screaming at me. Or Itzak torturing me about the budget. We can go when the filming's over.

ANNA. I'm coming too?

MOTL. Of course you are. I'll make the movies, and you'll act in them. Why are you looking at me like that?

ANNA. Motl...?

MOTL. *What?*

ANNA. Would you still want me to come if things were different?

MOTL. Different how?

ANNA. Well... if there wasn't any light under my skin, and I'd forgotten my magical language that everybody can understand? And if you were doing some boring job, and you got home every night to find me scratchy and dull because the baby had been screaming all day?

MOTL. But we won't have a baby.

ANNA. I will.

MOTL. What?

ANNA. I'm having a baby.

Pause.

What do you think?

MOTL. I think that...

ANNA. What?

MOTL. I think we'll manage.

ANNA. But it won't be how you imagined.

MOTL. No, it won't.

ANNA. It'll be all wrong.

Pause.

MOTL. Have you...?

ANNA. What are you thinking?

MOTL. Just that... in a place like this... where people are *trapped* by moral disapproval of one kind or another... only natural instincts can't be suppressed... because women are women and men are men...

ANNA. What are you talking about?

MOTL. ... Well, isn't there, perhaps, some wise old woman a girl can go to? I mean a *crone* with herbs and potions. Isn't that something people do?

ANNA. That's the most disgusting thing I've ever heard.

MOTL. Right, right.

ANNA. I'm not killing my baby.

MOTL. No, of course you aren't.

ANNA. It's the only family I've ever had.

MOTL. Exactly.

ANNA. Anyway, it's not up to you to decide.

MOTL. I know.

ANNA. It could be somebody else's.

MOTL. What?

ANNA. In fact it probably is.

MOTL. Whose?

ANNA. Jacob's.

MOTL. *Jacob's?*

He indicates the door.

That Jacob?

ANNA. Yes, obviously that Jacob.

MOTL. You said he never...

ANNA. It doesn't matter what I said.

Pause.

MOTL. Was it because of your part in the movie?

ANNA. No, of course it wasn't.

MOTL. Then *why*? Why *him*? Of all the people in the *world*?

She starts to cry.

ANNA. He wanted to. It wasn't important, not at all. I don't understand why people make such a fuss about it. As far as I can see, it's just something you do when you like somebody. And I like him. I do. He's funny and kind. He's clever too. You wouldn't be making this movie if it wasn't for him. And he's had most of the best ideas.

Pause.

I shouldn't have said that.

MOTL. No, you shouldn't.

ANNA. Still, I'm glad I did. You can go to America now. You'll make wonderful movies there, I know you will.

MOTL. What will you say to people here about the baby? So you don't get driven out of the village with sticks? And die in the snow?

ANNA. I'll think up a story.

MOTL. It'll need to be a good one.

ANNA. Any ideas?

MOTL. No.

ANNA. Nor me.

MOTL. I can stay if you want me to.

ANNA. I don't. I honestly don't. And I don't want to talk about it any more.

MOTL. All right.

She wraps up for her walk to the timber mill.

I love you.

ANNA. Yes, I know.

She goes. MOTL *remains where he is, stunned. After a few moments there's a knock at the door.*

MOTL. Anna?

He opens the door. It's JOSEF.

JOSEF. Sir?

MOTL. Yes, what is it?

JOSEF. I'm looking for Reb Bindel, sir. I was told he was here.

MOTL. He's gone back to the timber mill. What do you want?

JOSEF. I'm on my way to the station, sir. I've got to collect the new delivery.

MOTL: What's the problem?

JOSEF. I'll need some money to pay the stationmaster.

MOTL. I'd better give it to you myself, then.

JOSEF. If you would, sir.

　　MOTL finds a metal box.

MOTL. Itzak's cash box.

　　He tries to open it.

　　It's locked. Can you get it open?

JOSEF. If you say so, sir.

　　He finds a tool and starts forcing it open. MOTL *looks at the cinematograph-camera.*

MOTL. Josef?

JOSEF. Sir?

MOTL. Why don't I come to the station with you in the cart? I can keep you company on the way.

JOSEF. I'd like that, sir.

　　MOTL starts putting the cinematograph into its box.

　　Are you bringing the camera too?

MOTL. Yes, why not? We can show the stationmaster what we're doing. Does the express still come at dawn?

JOSEF. That's what I'm told, sir.

He has opened ITZAK's *cash box.*

I've got it open, sir.

MOTL. Fine, give it to me. (*Of the cinematograph.*) Can you carry this out?

JOSEF. Of course, sir.

He carries out the cinematograph in its box. MOTL *takes a few banknotes out of* ITZAK's *cash box. After a moment's thought, he stuffs the entire contents of the box, which is quite a large bunch of banknotes, into his pockets. He puts on his hat and coat, picks up anything else he really needs, and goes.*

Film: a train pulls into a station.

MAURICE. The express did me the favour of stopping. In fact, its status as an express turned out to be somewhat mythical, since it apparently always stopped. Crowds of peasants, fully expecting it to do so, climbed on board with their cargoes of geese and goats and carp in buckets. The sun was rising when the train pulled away from the station. With my camera poking out of the window...

Film: passing landscape.

...I filmed the birch trees... the telegraph wires... the snowdrifts... the horse-drawn ploughs... the waving children, the women bent over the furrows... all those pursuing memories that, in reality, I was never to see again.

End of film.

Scene Four

The studio. NATE *is reading from his script.*

NATE. 'EXT. TRAIN. DAWN. Anna runs desperately along the
tracks. Motl clasps her hand and, in a single athletic
movement, lifts her into the train.' INT. TRAIN. DAWN.
Anna looks adoringly into Motl's eyes. MOTL: "Anna, come
with me to America! I'm going to make you a star!" They
kiss. THE END.'

MAURICE. Yes, well, the screenplay takes some liberties with
the facts. Nobody wants a gloomy fade-out. There's no baby
in there either.

NATE. Are you saying there *was* a baby?

MAURICE. There was the *prospect* of a baby.

NATE. Who was the father?

MAURICE. I didn't know then and I don't know now.

NATE. Do you know what happened to Anna?

MAURICE. That, again, I couldn't tell you. Maybe she found a
husband. Maybe she went to a crone with herbs and potions.
Maybe she was driven out of the village with sticks and she
died in the snow.

NATE. Didn't you worry about her?

MAURICE. Look, I worry about her to this day.

NATE. Except she could have thought up a story.

MAURICE. That wouldn't be easy.

NATE. Believe me, Mr Montgomery, you never know what a
smart girl can come up with if she's stuck in a corner. What
if she told the Bindels…

MAURICE. …. that…?

NATE. ... she married their son Aron in secret before he went into the army, and now she's pregnant by him?

MAURICE. Don't you think that Aron might have something to say about that?

NATE. Not if he's been killed in battle.

MAURICE. Killed in battle? *That* would work. So his mother and father are...

NATE. ... they're overjoyed to know that they've got a grandchild on the way...

MAURICE. ... while Anna finally gets the family that she always wanted.

NATE. She converts, of course...

MAURICE. ... Of course, although I don't think anyone's too convinced by that...

NATE. ... and then she dies in childbirth.

MAURICE *looks at him, shocked.*

MAURICE. Did I hear you correctly?

NATE. Sure.

Pause.

MAURICE. Why must she die?

NATE. Because the focus of the story is on her daughter.

MAURICE. How do you know she had a daughter?

NATE. Because her daughter was my mother.

MAURICE. You're kidding, okay?

NATE. Look, it's all kidding.

Pause.

MAURICE. Go on.

NATE. Now we're in Brooklyn. Ida Bindel, elderly widow of Jacob the timber merchant...

MAURICE. So now you're killing off Jacob too?

NATE. Yes, and I'll tell you how it happens. One year after you leave, there is a big pogrom.

MAURICE. They were always big.

NATE. This was the biggest. The Cossacks rode through the village burning down every house they came to.

MAURICE. My father's studio?

NATE. I don't know about that.

MAURICE. Go on.

NATE. Jacob refused to leave the timber mill, so he burned to death inside it.

Pause.

MAURICE. Yes, I can see it. I can imagine it, I mean. Poor Jacob. I'm very sorry.

He takes out a handkerchief and wipes his eyes.

You were telling me about Ida.

NATE. Ida spends the last of her saved-up gold coins on taking herself and her baby granddaughter to New York. Her granddaughter gives birth to a baby boy.

MAURICE. What happened to *her*?

NATE. She disappears. Ida brings up the boy herself…

MAURICE. … and, as time goes by, she sends him to acting classes.

NATE. How did you know?

MAURICE. It's obvious. Cut to…

NATE. … caption: '1936.' Maurice Montgomery, visiting New York for a creative meeting, goes for an evening stroll through Greenwich Village…

MAURICE. … and it's raining. Pulls down his hat, turns up his collar. Hears the wail of a saxophone. He sees a modest theatre entrance with a glass-fronted case beside it. Photographs of the actors. One of the faces catches his attention. Could he have seen a face quite similar, years before, in his shaving mirror? On an impulse, he buys a ticket to see the play…

NATE. … meanwhile backstage it's all excitement. 'Maurice Montgomery's in tonight.' 'Who invited him?' 'What is he casting?' Nathan Dershowitz, making his first entrance, carrying the bottle of contraband medicine that he's brought for his dying mother, blinded by the lights, sees only the face of his future in row G.

MAURICE. This is the fade-out?

NATE. *No!* A painted sign. 'Stage Door.' The show is over. Two men huddle beneath the awning. 'Mr Dershowitz,' says Maurice Montgomery, 'I have one final movie to make. I want to test you for the leading role.' Which, as I remember, is how it was.

MAURICE. It's how it *sort* of was, but there's a hole in the plot through which you could drive a Greyhound bus.

NATE. What's that?

MAURICE. If you are my grandson, why have you waited till now to tell me? Why not then and there, beneath the awning at the stage door?

NATE. Because your grandson is the last person on earth who you would test for a leading role. Or am I wrong?

MAURICE. No, no, it's very perceptive of you. Since I was fifteen years of age, I've run as fast as I could from my family, and the people who loved me, and the people who made me what I am.

Tears come to his eyes.

I've had no deep attachments. I've avoided them, or fled them. The only thing that I've really cared about is movies. I'm not proud of it. It may even be that I'll go to my grave repenting of my guilt, but what can I do? I made my choice. It can't be helped.

NATE. No redemption at the fade-out?

MAURICE. None.

NATE. How about this?

MAURICE. I'm listening.

> NATE *sits and looks at* MAURICE *with some intensity.*

NATE. Nick Driver, still Nate Dershowitz at heart, fixes
Maurice Montgomery with a compassionate eye. 'When I
was a boy,' he says, 'my great-grandmother Ida would say to
me, "Nathan, put on your good shirt, we're giving ourselves
a treat." We'd go the Alhambra movie house, she'd buy me
an ice-cream soda and we saw every movie there that you
ever made. Nazimova in *The Singing of the Angel.* Gloria
Swanson as the girl who was deaf and dumb, only she's
healed by the power of prayer. Then the talkies. Joel McCrea
in the cowboy movie…

MAURICE. *One Man Alone.*

NATE. *One Man Alone.* Barbara Stanwyck in *I Married a
Demon.* Freddie Bartholomew as the violin prodigy. Dick
Powell and Ruby Keeler as the boy and girl in the hat shop
who hate each other, but they get married in the end. Ida
would say, 'If only Jacob was alive! How proud he would be
to know that Motl Mendl is making Jewish movies.'

> *Pause.*

Too schmaltzy?

MAURICE. It's absurdly schmaltzy but I'll buy it. Thank you.

NATE. It's a pleasure.

> NATE *goes.* MAURICE *walks into the set, shutting the door
> behind him. Looks at the cinematograph. As though
> transformed by a magician, the set becomes, no longer the
> studio set, but the original photographic studio.*
>
> *Snow is seen falling outside the window and a fire flickers in
> the grate.*

TSIPPA *comes in, goes to the cupboard and takes out a loaf of bread. Places it on the table, then lays out a pair of candles.*

MAURICE *himself takes out four plates, knives and forks and lays them on the table for* TSIPPA, *himself and two guests. Then a bottle and four glasses.*

There's a knock on the door. It's JACOB *and* IDA. TSIPPA *lets them in and they enter, touching the mezuzah with a kiss as they pass.* IDA *and* TSIPPA *kiss.* MAURICE *and* IDA *kiss.* JACOB *and* MAURICE *embrace.*

At the table, JACOB *gives* MAURICE – *who doesn't have one – a yarmulke.*

TSIPPA *lights the candles, then gestures a welcome to the Shabbos and places her hands over her eyes.*

As everyone sits…

The End.